MAJOR WORLD LEADERS

KING ABDULLAH II
YASIR ARAFAT
BASHAR al-ASSAD
MENACHEM BEGIN
SILVIO BERLUSCONI
TONY BLAIR
GEORGE W. BUSH
JIMMY CARTER
FIDEL CASTRO
RECEP TAYYIP ERDOĞAN
VICENTE FOX
SADDAM HUSSEIN
HAMID KARZAI
KIM IL SUNG AND KIM JONG IL
HOSNI MUBARAK
PERVEZ MUSHARRAF
VLADIMIR PUTIN
MOHAMMED REZA PAHLAVI
ANWAR SADAT
THE SAUDI ROYAL FAMILY
GERHARD SCHROEDER
ARIEL SHARON
LUIZ INÁCIO LULA DA SILVA
MUAMMAR QADDAFI

MAJOR WORLD LEADERS

King Abdullah II

Heather Lehr Wagner

Philadelphia

Cover: King Abdullah II of Jordan, in full dress military uniform, on a visit to Spain, October 20, 1999.

Frontispiece: King Abdullah II of Jordan addresses the United Nations General Assembly during the UN Millennium Summit, September 6, 2000, in New York.

CHELSEA HOUSE PUBLISHERS

V.P., NEW PRODUCT DEVELOPMENT Sally Cheney
DIRECTOR OF PRODUCTION Kim Shinners
CREATIVE MANAGER Takeshi Takahashi
MANUFACTURING MANAGER Diann Grasse

Staff for KING ABDULLAH II

EXECUTIVE EDITOR Lee Marcott
EDITORIAL ASSISTANT Carla Greenberg
PRODUCTION EDITOR Noelle Nardone
PHOTO EDITOR Sarah Bloom
INTERIOR DESIGN Takeshi Takahashi
COVER DESIGN Keith Trego
LAYOUT 21st Century Publishing and Communications, Inc.

©2005 by Chelsea House Publishers, a subsidiary of Haights Cross Communications. All rights reserved. Printed and bound in China.

A Haights Cross Communications Company

http://www.chelseahouse.com

First Printing

1 3 5 7 9 8 6 4 2

Library of Congress Cataloging-in-Publication Data

Wagner, Heather Lehr.
　King Abdullah II / Heather Lehr Wagner.
　　p. cm.—(Major world leaders)
Includes index.
　ISBN 0-7910-8259-8 (hardcover)
　1. Jordan—Juvenile literature. 2. Abdullah II, King of Jordan, 1962–　—Juvenile literature. I. Title. II. Series.
DS153.W34 2005
956.9504'4'092—dc22

2004023509

All links and web addresses were checked and verified to be correct at the time of publication. Because of the dynamic nature of the web, some addresses and links may have changed since publication and may no longer be valid.

TABLE OF CONTENTS

	Foreword: On Leadership Arthur M. Schlesinger, jr.	6
1	Long Live the King	12
2	A Kingdom Carved From the Desert	22
3	A Trial Kingdom	40
4	Early Years in an Unstable Time	56
5	An American Education	69
6	The New King	83
7	A Vision of Change	98
	Chronology	108
	Further Reading	109
	Index	110

On Leadership

Arthur M. Schlesinger, jr.

Leadership, it may be said, is really what makes the world go round. Love no doubt smoothes the passage; but love is a private transaction between consenting adults. Leadership is a public transaction with history. The idea of leadership affirms the capacity of individuals to move, inspire, and mobilize masses of people so that they act together in pursuit of an end. Sometimes leadership serves good purposes, sometimes bad; but whether the end is benign or evil, great leaders are those men and women who leave their personal stamp on history.

Now, the very concept of leadership implies the proposition that individuals can make a difference. This proposition has never been universally accepted. From classical times to the present day, eminent thinkers have regarded individuals as no more than the agents and pawns of larger forces, whether the gods and goddesses of the ancient world or, in the modern era, race, class, nation, the dialectic, the will of the people, the spirit of the times, history itself. Against such forces, the individual dwindles into insignificance.

So contends the thesis of historical determinism. Tolstoy's great novel *War and Peace* offers a famous statement of the case. Why, Tolstoy asked, did millions of men in the Napoleonic Wars, denying their human feelings and their common sense, move back and forth across Europe slaughtering their fellows? "The war," Tolstoy answered, "was bound to happen simply because it was bound to happen." All prior history determined it. As for leaders, they, Tolstoy said, "are but the labels that serve to give a name to an end and, like labels, they have the least possible connection with the event." The greater the leader, "the more conspicuous the inevitability and the predestination of every act he commits." The leader, said Tolstoy, is "the slave of history."

Determinism takes many forms. Marxism is the determinism of class. Nazism the determinism of race. But the idea of men and women as the slaves of history runs athwart the deepest human instincts. Rigid determinism abolishes the idea of human freedom—the assumption of free choice that underlies every move we make, every word we speak, every thought we think. It abolishes the idea of human responsibility, since it is manifestly unfair to reward or punish people for actions that are by definition beyond their control. No one can live consistently by any deterministic creed. The Marxist states prove this themselves by their extreme susceptibility to the cult of leadership.

More than that, history refutes the idea that individuals make no difference. In December 1931 a British politician crossing Fifth Avenue in New York City between 76th and 77th Streets around 10:30 P.M. looked in the wrong direction and was knocked down by an automobile—a moment, he later recalled, of a man aghast, a world aglare: "I do not understand why I was not broken like an eggshell or squashed like a gooseberry." Fourteen months later an American politician, sitting in an open car in Miami, Florida, was fired on by an assassin; the man beside him was hit. Those who believe that individuals make no difference to history might well ponder whether the next two decades would have been the same had Mario Constasino's car killed Winston Churchill in 1931 and Giuseppe Zangara's bullet killed Franklin Roosevelt in 1933. Suppose, in addition, that Lenin had died of typhus in Siberia in 1895 and that Hitler had been killed on the Western Front in 1916. What would the 20th century have looked like now?

For better or for worse, individuals do make a difference. "The notion that a people can run itself and its affairs anonymously," wrote the philosopher William James, "is now well known to be the silliest of absurdities. Mankind does nothing save through initiatives on the part of inventors, great or small, and imitation by the rest of us—these are the sole factors in human progress. Individuals of genius show the way, and set the patterns, which common people then adopt and follow."

Leadership, James suggests, means leadership in thought as well as in action. In the long run, leaders in thought may well make the greater difference to the world. "The ideas of economists and political philosophers, both when they are right and when they are wrong," wrote John Maynard Keynes, "are more powerful than is commonly understood. Indeed the world is ruled by little else. Practical men, who believe themselves to be quite exempt from any intellectual influences, are usually the slaves of some defunct economist. . . . The power of vested interests is vastly exaggerated compared with the gradual encroachment of ideas."

But, as Woodrow Wilson once said, "Those only are leaders of men, in the general eye, who lead in action.... It is at their hands that new thought gets its translation into the crude language of deeds." Leaders in thought often invent in solitude and obscurity, leaving to later generations the tasks of imitation. Leaders in action—the leaders portrayed in this series—have to be effective in their own time.

And they cannot be effective by themselves. They must act in response to the rhythms of their age. Their genius must be adapted, in a phrase from William James, "to the receptivities of the moment." Leaders are useless without followers. "There goes the mob," said the French politician, hearing a clamor in the streets. "I am their leader. I must follow them." Great leaders turn the inchoate emotions of the mob to purposes of their own. They seize on the opportunities of their time, the hopes, fears, frustrations, crises, potentialities. They succeed when events have prepared the way for them, when the community is awaiting to be aroused, when they can provide the clarifying and organizing ideas. Leadership completes the circuit between the individual and the mass and thereby alters history.

It may alter history for better or for worse. Leaders have been responsible for the most extravagant follies and most monstrous crimes that have beset suffering humanity. They have also been vital in such gains as humanity has made in individual freedom, religious and racial tolerance, social justice, and respect for human rights.

There is no sure way to tell in advance who is going to lead for good and who for evil. But a glance at the gallery of men and women in MAJOR WORLD LEADERS suggests some useful tests.

One test is this: Do leaders lead by force or by persuasion? By command or by consent? Through most of history leadership was exercised by the divine right of authority. The duty of followers was to defer and to obey. "Theirs not to reason why/Theirs but to do and die." On occasion, as with the so-called enlightened despots of the 18th century in Europe, absolutist leadership was animated by humane purposes. More often, absolutism nourished the passion for domination, land, gold, and conquest and resulted in tyranny.

The great revolution of modern times has been the revolution of equality. "Perhaps no form of government," wrote the British historian James Bryce in his study of the United States, *The American Commonwealth*, "needs great leaders so much as democracy." The idea that all people should be equal in their legal condition has undermined the old structure of authority, hierarchy, and deference. The revolution of equality has had two contrary effects on the nature of leadership. For equality, as Alexis de Tocqueville pointed out in his great study *Democracy in America*, might mean equality in servitude as well as equality in freedom.

"I know of only two methods of establishing equality in the political world," Tocqueville wrote. "Rights must be given to every citizen, or none at all to anyone . . . save one, who is the master of all." There was no middle ground "between the sovereignty of all and the absolute power of one man." In his astonishing prediction of 20th-century totalitarian dictatorship, Tocqueville explained how the revolution of equality could lead to the *Führerprinzip* and more terrible absolutism than the world had ever known.

But when rights are given to every citizen and the sovereignty of all is established, the problem of leadership takes a new form, becomes more exacting than ever before. It is easy to issue commands and enforce them by the rope and the stake, the concentration camp and the *gulag*. It is much harder to use argument and achievement to overcome opposition and win consent. The Founding Fathers of the United States understood the difficulty. They believed that history had given them the opportunity to decide, as Alexander Hamilton wrote in the first Federalist Paper, whether men are indeed capable of basing government on "reflection and choice, or whether they are forever destined to depend . . . on accident and force."

Government by reflection and choice called for a new style of leadership and a new quality of followership. It required leaders to be responsive to popular concerns, and it required followers to be active and informed participants in the process. Democracy does not eliminate emotion from politics; sometimes it fosters demagoguery; but it is confident that, as the greatest of democratic leaders put it, you cannot fool all of the people all of the time. It measures leadership by results and retires those who overreach or falter or fail.

It is true that in the long run despots are measured by results too. But they can postpone the day of judgment, sometimes indefinitely, and in the meantime they can do infinite harm. It is also true that democracy is no guarantee of virtue and intelligence in government, for the voice of the people is not necessarily the voice of God. But democracy, by assuring the right of opposition, offers built-in resistance to the evils inherent in absolutism. As the theologian Reinhold Niebuhr summed it up, "Man's capacity for justice makes democracy possible, but man's inclination to justice makes democracy necessary."

A second test for leadership is the end for which power is sought. When leaders have as their goal the supremacy of a master race or the promotion of totalitarian revolution or the acquisition and exploitation of colonies or the protection of greed and privilege or the preservation of personal power, it is likely that their leadership will do little to advance the cause of humanity. When their goal is the abolition of slavery, the liberation of women, the enlargement of opportunity for the poor and powerless, the extension of equal rights to racial minorities, the defense of the freedoms of expression and opposition, it is likely that their leadership will increase the sum of human liberty and welfare.

Leaders have done great harm to the world. They have also conferred great benefits. You will find both sorts in this series. Even "good" leaders must be regarded with a certain wariness. Leaders are not demigods; they put on their trousers one leg after another just like ordinary mortals. No leader is infallible, and every leader needs to be reminded of this at regular intervals. Irreverence irritates leaders but is their salvation. Unquestioning submission corrupts leaders and demeans followers. Making a cult of a leader is always a mistake. Fortunately hero worship generates its own antidote. "Every hero," said Emerson, "becomes a bore at last."

The signal benefit the great leaders confer is to embolden the rest of us to live according to our own best selves, to be active, insistent, and resolute in affirming our own sense of things. For great leaders attest to the reality of human freedom against the supposed inevitabilities of history. And they attest to the wisdom and power that may lie within the most unlikely of us, which is why Abraham Lincoln remains the supreme example of great leadership. A great leader, said Emerson, exhibits new possibilities to all humanity. "We feed on genius. . . . Great men exist that there may be greater men."

Great leaders, in short, justify themselves by emancipating and empowering their followers. So humanity struggles to master its destiny, remembering with Alexis de Tocqueville: "It is true that around every man a fatal circle is traced beyond which he cannot pass; but within the wide verge of that circle he is powerful and free; as it is with man, so with communities."

CHAPTER 1

Long Live the King

For months, one of the chief topics of political gossip in Jordan had been the question of who would become the next king. Ever since King Hussein left his country in the middle of 1998 to travel to the Mayo Clinic in the United States for treatment of lymphatic cancer, speculation had grown about the state of his health and about who would rule the nation after his death.

It was difficult for most Jordanians to imagine their country without King Hussein as its ruler. He had been king of the Middle Eastern nation since 1952 and now, some 46 years later, his fate seemed inextricably linked with the fate of the land he ruled. As King Hussein endured month after month of grueling chemotherapy treatments at the respected Mayo Clinic's location in Rochester, Minnesota, his people wondered when—and if—he would be coming home.

Long Live the King   13

King Hussein gestures after being asked for news on the Camp David peace accords. After spending years working toward an international peace conference that would include many Arab countries, King Hussein was not invited to the accords, arranged by U.S. President Jimmy Carter. Only Egyptian President Anwar Sadat and Israeli Prime Minister Menachem Begin attended. Hussein appears with British Prime Minister James Callaghan (left), in this September 1978 photo.

The question of who would rule after Hussein should not have sparked such fierce debate. King Hussein himself had already answered the question—he had, in fact, answered it 33 years earlier, when he had named his youngest brother, Hassan, crown prince. The 51-year-old Hassan was currently acting as regent while King Hussein underwent cancer treatment, providing him with an opportunity to demonstrate his ability to rule in his brother's absence.

King Hussein had underscored his brother's role as crown prince well before his illness, including his brother in certain critical matters for Jordan's policymaking, such as the difficult negotiations of a peace treaty with Israel in the early 1990s. Hussein had, on several occasions, emphasized his wish that Hassan would succeed him to the throne. Even as he prepared for cancer treatment at the Mayo Clinic, he told Randa Habib, correspondent for Radio Monte Carlo and Agence France Presse, that the succession "rests in the hands of my brother (His Royal Highness Crown Prince El Hassan), whom I have chosen over others many years ago, and who has shouldered his responsibilities and performed his duties fully." The king went on to state, "All the issues that may be surrounded by speculation or anxiety will have the right answers in the right time."

Despite the ill king's firm expression of confidence in his younger brother, speculation continued. Rumors appeared in the international press hinting of competition among members of the royal family for the right to rule Jordan.

Although King Hussein named his youngest brother as crown prince, it required an amendment to Jordan's Constitution in order to do so. The Constitution had initially required for the throne to pass from father to son, with the eldest son becoming ruler upon his father's death. King Hussein did have a son—in fact, he had five of them. When Hussein's first son, Abdullah, was born in 1962, he had been declared the crown prince. But in the early 1960s, the political climate in Jordan was very unstable, and threats against Hussein made his early death at the hands of assassins seem a very real possibility. In 1965, he decided to name his youngest brother Hassan his successor.

King Hussein's belief was that his brother would be better able to hold together the kingdom than a child. And the role of

Long Live the King   15

King Hussein and his family in 1968: his wife, Princess Muna, and son, Prince Abdullah. Abdullah was Hussein's first son (one of five), and he achieved succession when Hussein named him Crown Prince just before his death in 1999. Jordan's constitutional provision for primogeniture (succession by the firstborn son) also supported the choice.

king was a critical one for the Jordanian government. As a monarchy, Jordan's king appoints almost all members of the government and judiciary, with the exception of the lower house of representatives, which is elected by the people. The king has the ability to open, close, suspend, or even dissolve the legislature. He holds the power to command Jordan's armed forces, approve laws, sign treaties, declare war, and conclude peace with other nations.

With such a broad scope of powers at his command, it was perhaps not surprising that the king's succession was a matter viewed seriously both within and outside Jordan's borders. Consequently, it was not surprising that the question should be raised now that the king's sons were no longer children, but young men with unique ambitions and abilities.

THE CHILDREN OF HUSSEIN

King Hussein's family included children from four different marriages. His first wife had been Sharifa Dina bin Abdul Hamid (Queen Dina), a distant cousin who was seven years older than the king. That marriage lasted 18 months, and from it came a daughter, Alia.

In 1961, King Hussein married a young Englishwoman, Antoinette Gardiner (later known as Princess Muna). They had two sons, Abdullah and Feisal, and twin daughters, Zein and Aisha. They divorced after 11 years of marriage, and King Hussein married Alia Toukan. Princess Alia was a Palestinian, an important factor in a nation whose population contains nearly as many Palestinians as Jordanians. Hussein and Alia had two children: a daughter named Haya and a son, Ali. They also adopted a young Palestinian girl, Abir. Princess Alia was killed in a helicopter crash after only four years of marriage. In 1978, King Hussein married 26-year-old Lisa Halaby (who became known as Queen Noor), an Arab American, with whom he had two sons—Hamzah and Hashim—and two daughters, Iman and Raiyah.

Long Live the King

The wedding of King Hussein and Antoinette Gardiner, from Ipswich, England, who afterward took the name Princess Muna ("Delight"). Gardiner was Hussein's second wife.

In addition to these complicated stepfamily dynamics, there were others whose link to the throne was being debated as the question of succession arose. Crown Prince Hassan himself had four children, including one son, Prince Rashid. The king's other brother, Prince Muhammad, had sons also, and his oldest, Prince Talal, had formed a strong bond with King Hussein and was viewed as yet another candidate for the throne.

In 1978, the king had gone one step further and specified in writing to Crown Prince Hassan not only that he would succeed Hussein, but who Hassan's successor should be: Hussein's third son, Prince Ali. But now, nearly 20 years later, facing a life-threatening illness, many believed that the king might change his mind.

There had been growing signs that the king had a new favorite among his sons: Prince Hamzah, his son with his fourth wife, Queen Noor. In 1997, when Hamzah turned 18, his father had issued a public "letter" to Hamzah, stating his belief that his son would go on to "great achievements," and also noting that he himself had been 18 years old when he had become king. The letter had sparked speculation that Prince Hamzah would soon become the king's choice for his heir, and the onset of Hussein's cancer treatment, less than a year later, added fuel to the speculation.

It was a complicated situation in a country that had known essentially only two rulers in its entire history. Hussein's grandfather, King Abdullah, had ruled the land when the territory first known as Transjordan was set aside by British forces from the desert sands to the east of the Jordan River in 1921. For 30 years King Abdullah shaped a kingdom from the loosely defined borders designated by the British and others, until his assassination while saying his Friday prayers at a mosque in Jerusalem. By his side as the king was gunned down was his 16-year-old grandson, Hussein.

Hussein became crown prince and his father, Talal, became Jordan's new king, but his rule would last only a year. Suffering from schizophrenia, Talal was removed from the throne by a vote in Parliament after being examined by five doctors (three Jordanian and two foreign) and determined unfit to rule. Hussein's mother, Queen Zein, served as regent following her husband's hospitalization abroad and abdication, until her son turned 18 and was crowned king. The reign of Abdullah had lasted 30 years; that of his grandson, Hussein, some 46 years. But now, many believed, that reign was coming to an end.

RETURN OF THE KING

In January 1999 King Hussein completed his treatment at the Mayo Clinic and returned to Jordan, declaring that his health was improving. But many who saw him were shocked at his gaunt, haggard appearance and questioned his claims of improved physical condition.

Only hours after his return, the king made an attempt to diminish the speculation about his succession, but at the same time did not offer the firm endorsement of his brother, Hassan, that he had made six months earlier. Rumors increased that 18-year-old Prince Hamzah would be named successor, sparking whispered criticisms of American-born Queen Noor's efforts to advance the future of her son.

Finally, on January 25, 1999, only days after his return to Jordan, the king announced that his oldest son, Prince Abdullah, would once more be named crown prince, as he had been for the first three years of his life. King Hussein noted that the Jordanian Constitution had originally specified *primogeniture*—succession by the eldest son—and he intended to honor this policy. King Hussein further noted that, should Abdullah succeed him to the throne, Abdullah's crown prince must be Prince Hamzah.

The 36-year-old Abdullah was a logical choice for crown prince. He had built a promising career in the Jordanian military, rising to the rank of major general and commanding the elite Special Forces unit responsible for Jordan's internal security. Abdullah had performed heroically during riots in southern Jordan in 1996. He was mature and well educated, and had a Palestinian wife.

Still, King Hussein felt he needed to explain his choice. The 63-year-old king wrote a letter to Hassan, a letter that he then publicly released for broadcast on Jordanian television. The letter noted that King Hussein was disappointed with his brother's performance during his six-month absence, citing a crisis in the army that he had had to resolve while undergoing chemotherapy, and accusing his brother of favoritism and launching a smear campaign against Queen Noor and her children. The letter included a statement

Queen Noor and King Hussein, arriving in Paris. Noor, Hussein's fourth wife, is an Arab American (born Lisa Halaby) and holds a degree in urban planning from Princeton University. They met through her father, Najeeb, who collaborated with Hussein on Jordanian aviation projects.

in favor of Prince Hamzah, and an ardent defense of his fourth wife:

> As for Noor, she brought happiness to me and cared for me during my illness, with the utmost loving affection. She, the Jordanian, who belongs to this country with every fibre of her being, holds her head high in the defence and service of this country's interest. She is the mother who devotes all her efforts to her family.

The letter contained King Hussein's explanation for why he had first named Hassan as his successor, and offered clues about his decision to now name Abdullah as crown prince:

> At the time my decision concerning succession to the throne was not subject to any personal or emotional considerations but rather was a national one. It was a decision stemming from my feeling of responsibility and the need to place the national interests and the country's stability and survival above all considerations and interests. My objective was to perform my duty towards my people and nation, to seek God's blessing and peace of mind, and to achieve stability and reassure all Jordanians about the future.

Only hours after appointing Abdullah as his successor, King Hussein boarded a plane to return to the Mayo Clinic. Tests had revealed that his cancer had returned. He was placed in the Intensive Care Unit and embarked on a new and more invasive route of chemotherapy. His health quickly began to fail, however, and he slipped into a coma.

Queen Noor decided that if her husband was losing his battle against cancer, it should not be lost in Rochester, Minnesota. Within hours, the king, his family, ten physicians, a flight nurse, a respiratory therapist, and the necessary medical equipment and medications were loaded onto a plane bound for Jordan. Upon his return, King Hussein was placed on life-support equipment at the medical center named in his honor in Jordan's capital city, Amman.

On February 7, 1999 during noon prayers, King Hussein was pronounced dead, while surrounded by his children and relatives. Queen Noor turned to her stepson, Abdullah, and said, "The King has died; long live the King."

CHAPTER 2

A Kingdom Carved From the Desert

The Hashemite Kingdom of Jordan occupies a land rich in history, and its desert sands have witnessed centuries of conquest. The Greeks and Romans once marked Jordan as part of their empires. Both Muslims and Christians invaded the land and claimed it for their own.

It is a land whose archeological sites bear witness to those who have come before. Important figures from the religions of Islam, Judaism, and Christianity once crossed its terrain. It is believed that the Prophet Muhammad traveled through Jordan. Lot hid from God's wrathful vengeance against Sodom and Gomorrah in Jordan, and Moses and his brother, Aaron, died there. Jesus was baptized in Jordan's large river, and the man who performed the ceremony, John the Baptist, was beheaded there.

A Kingdom Carved From the Desert

Camels in the Jordan River valley, near Jiftlich. Because of the harsh desert conditions throughout much of Jordan, over the centuries much of the country's population, especially Bedouin tribes, have practiced nomadic and seminomadic herding or subsistence farming to eke out a meager living from the land.

Although nearly 85 percent of Jordan consists of desert, it is a rich and varied landscape, stretching from the red sands and tall cliffs of the south to olive groves of the north. The Dead Sea—the lowest point on earth—lies within Jordan, while the brilliant coral reefs of the Red Sea lie to its south. In the center of the country is a land rich with wheat fields, surrounded by canyons and mountains.

The kingdom of Jordan occupies a land slightly smaller in size than the state of Indiana. Yet is location has made it a critical player in Middle Eastern politics. To its west lie Israel and the West Bank territories. To Jordan's north is Syria; its eastern edge borders Iraq. To its south lies Saudi Arabia. This location—in the very heart of the Middle East—has forced the kingdom and its rulers to assume an often-critical diplomatic role in resolving the tensions in the region.

It is ironic that those who first shaped the borders that would initially define the land called "Transjordan" had in mind precisely that role for this small stretch of desert. The Europeans who carved the Middle East into different nations and zones of influence after World War I viewed Jordan as a buffer, a safe ally for European—specifically British—interests in the region.

UNDER OTTOMAN RULE

The man who survived palace intrigue to become the king of Jordan in 1999 was Abdullah bin Al Hussein, the eldest son of the late King Hussein, and the forty-third generation direct descendant of the Prophet Muhammad. He was born in Amman, Jordan, on January 30, 1962, to King Hussein and his second wife, the former Antoinette Gardiner, an Englishwoman who took the name Princess Muna when she converted to Islam at the time of her marriage.

The story of King Abdullah's reign begins well before 1999, however. To understand the reign of King Abdullah II, it is important to first understand the politics and personalities that brought the Hashemite family to power in Jordan.

In the early part of the twentieth century, much of the Middle East formed part of the vast Ottoman Empire. The Ottomans spoke Turkish and followed Islam; they began their conquest in the fourteenth century, traveling west from central and northeast Asia and conquering the lands over which they traveled. Their empire gradually contained portions of Europe,

A Kingdom Carved From the Desert

the Balkan Peninsula, and lands once controlled by the Serbs, the Bulgurs, and the Macedonians. By 1453, the Ottomans had captured the city of Constantinople (in modern Turkey), and made this city linking Europe and Asia their capital.

For several centuries, the Ottomans ruled over their vast empire, equal in size to the continental United States. In the 1500s and 1600s it would be the most powerful empire in the world, spreading from Asia into Europe and northern Africa, and encompassing much of the Middle East. The Ottomans joined the many lands of their territory under a single political system. Educated, professional religious leaders were granted specific powers over specific regions. They all reported to a single, supreme religious authority—the *caliph*, or sultan, based in Constantinople. The caliph was believed to be the successor to the prophet Muhammad, and the moral leader for the more than 100 million Muslims.

But such absolute power inevitably led to corruption. Sultans frequently seized the throne from family members, either murdering them or forcing them into exile. Citizens in the empire were divided into two groups or classes. The upper class (the imperial family, wealthy landowners, religious leaders, military leaders) paid no taxes. The lower class (farmers, craftsmen, peasants) paid heavy taxes to support the luxurious lifestyles of their rulers.

Gradually, pieces of the Ottoman Empire began to slip away. By the twentieth century, strategically important territories had been lost to Greece, and Great Britain was occupying Egypt. Europeans had brought Western ideas and Western influences to the region. Political groups were secretly organizing, plotting revolution.

As Ottoman authorities focused on maintaining their hold on their most important lands, and military divisions were sent to patrol strategically important regions, little thought was given to the lands beyond the Jordan River. The population of the territory was small, and scattered. The climate was harsh;

there was little opportunity for any kind of development of the land. Those people who lived there carved out a subsistence existence for the most part, managing to produce enough food for themselves to eat, but with little left over for any kind of economic growth. In the north, peasant tribes clustered around villages. On the edge of the desert, Bedouin tribes herded livestock, traveling with their herds as the demands for grazing and water led them.

This land truly was on the edge of the empire, of interest more for those passing through it than for any opportunities the land itself offered. British explorer Gertrude Bell, an extraordinary 31-year-old woman who spoke Arabic and traveled alone through much of the Middle East, passed into the region around 1900, writing with pleasure of crossing the narrow Jordan River into the Jordan Valley and finding colorful fields in the midst of the arid wilderness. She described the yellow daisies, dark purple onions, tiny blue iris, red anemone, and "the sheets and sheets of varied and exquisite color."

Bell traveled on to the Roman ruins of the city of Petra—the hidden city that had once been the capital of the Nabateans and had played an important role in desert trade, but had, over the centuries, been buried in the desert sand. The entrance to the ruins was a great arch of red sandstone rocks, some 100 feet high, and inside was a temple carved from pink rock. Inside the ruins were 750 tombs, some soaring three stories high. Bell camped among the tombs, later writing of the beauty of the Corinthian columns that soared, "upwards to the very top of the cliff in the most exquisite proportions, carved with groups of figures almost as fresh as when the chisel left them—all this in the rose red rock, with the sun just touching it and making it look almost transparent."

Bell was one of the few travelers intrepid enough to brave the desert journey to view the wonders of Petra, however. A few hardy archeologists and traders traversed the land, but their numbers were small. It is not surprising that Ottoman authorities, focused on retaining control of the critical pieces of their empire, had little resources to spare for an arid desert with few people and fewer prospects.

REVOLUTION AND REVOLT

In the early 1900s, revolution struck the Ottoman Empire. A growing movement for independence was sweeping through the lands. Parts of the empire had been lost, and other territories were quietly beginning to take steps to achieve their own liberation from Ottoman rule. This was welcome news to the British authorities in the region, who were eager to extend their influence from Cairo to more of the Middle East, protecting the passage to their so-called crown jewel of India. British authorities were also aware of the possibility of oil that portions of the Middle East offered, and determined to quietly hasten the crumbling of the Ottoman Empire.

There were many leaders in the region secretly seeking an alliance with the British in their efforts to overthrow the Ottomans and carve out their own kingdoms. Chief among these was the ruler of the holy Muslim city of Mecca on the Arabian Peninsula, Sharif Hussein. Hussein, in control of one of the holiest cities to all Muslims, could conceivably challenge the moral authority of the Ottoman caliph, and his sons, Abdullah and Faisal, were soon negotiating with the British to help spark an "Arab revolt" against Ottoman rule.

In 1914, Sharif Hussein's second son, Abdullah, met with a British delegate in Cairo. After a lengthy discussion that touched upon Arabian history and poetry, Abdullah gradually hinted that a gift of British machine guns might help Arabian forces to guard against an attack by the Turkish military. Britain was interested—interested enough to continue to meet with Abdullah and his brother on numerous occasions—but not yet ready to openly arm a rebellion against the Ottoman rulers.

Clearly, Sharif Hussein might be a strong enough ally to successfully challenge Ottoman authority. As sharif, Hussein was believed to be a direct descendant of Muhammad. As guardian of the holy city of Mecca, Hussein was responsible not only for guarding the city, but also for hosting and managing the *hajj*, the pilgrimage to Mecca that all Muslims are called to make at least once in their life. It was a powerful—and lucrative—position. Hussein's family had been granted the honor of this function many years ago. They were descendants of Hashem, known as "Hashemites."

The Ottoman sultan had sensed the threat posed by Sharif Hussein, and had invited him to be his "guest" (essentially an excuse for keeping him hostage and under surveillance) for much of his life in Constantinople. Once back in Arabia, Hussein was far from secure—much of his territory was being challenged by another Arab, Ibn Saud of Riyadh. The Saudis and the Hashemites shared a hatred of the Ottoman forces, but this was one of the few things they held in common. Since 1910, they had been fighting sporadically for control of Arabian territory and were equally powerful.

This was yet another reason why the British hesitated when choosing to back an Arabian-led revolt against the Ottomans. Choosing to back Sharif Hussein and his four sons would mean alienating the powerful Ibn Saud. But the sons made a strong impression on the British with whom they attempted to negotiate.

Abdullah was persistent in his efforts to win British support for a revolt against the Turks. Gradually, he led the British to believe that the rival leaders in Arabia were unifying behind the leadership of his father to form an Arabia "for all Arabs." This was a more attractive prospect for Britain as the threat of war with the Ottoman Empire gradually seemed more likely, and by 1914 Britain's War Minister, Lord Kitchener, ordered that Abdullah be informed, "If the Arab nation assist England in this war that has been forced upon us by Turkey, England will guarantee that no internal intervention take place in Arabia, and will give Arabs [meaning those who lived in Arabia] every assistance against foreign aggression."

A Kingdom Carved From the Desert

Lord Kitchener felt his message was quite clear, but the British foreign office changed its meaning when translating it into Arabic, pledging British support for "the emancipation of all Arabs," a much broader pledge than that which had originally been intended. Later British pledges were directed to nearly all of Arabic-speaking Asia (including Palestine, Syria and Mesopotamia), promising to their residents that if they revolted against the Turks, Britain would recognize and guarantee their independence.

It is not surprising that Sharif Hussein and his sons viewed these pledges as indications that Britain would stand beside them in a revolt against the Ottomans. But far more critical to the development of the contemporary Middle East was a series of letters between Sharif Hussein and Sir Henry McMahon, who would succeed Lord Kitchener in Cairo as Consul-General. Ten letters, five from each side, would be exchanged between July 1915 and January 1916. These letters would trigger what became known as the Arab Revolt, would eventually provide Hussein and three of his sons with kingdoms to rule, and would dramatically transform the Middle East.

WAR AND DIVISION

In his correspondence with McMahon, Hussein spelled out his desire for a kingdom far greater than the Arabian Peninsula—a kingdom that would encompass all Arab-speaking people. But what precisely he was promised was the subject of great dispute. While there is little doubt that Sharif Hussein was promised an independent Hijaz region—the territory in Arabia that surrounded Mecca—he believed that he would become "king of the Arabs." But the boundaries of this kingdom were never formally determined. Its borders were never set down on a map.

Hussein believed that his kingdom would be, in fact, a vast Islamic empire, stretching north into Palestine, south to the Persian Gulf, and containing the territories of Syria and

Mesopotamia (modern-day Iraq). But the British had little intention of creating a large Islamic empire that might pose a threat to their own control of the vast Muslim population of India. Unbeknownst to Hussein, Britain was also negotiating secretly with the French, carving up the Middle East into "zones of influence" well before the war with the Ottoman Empire was over.

Representing the British in these negotiations was Sir Mark Sykes. The French negotiator was François Georges Picot. While Sykes was aware of—and, in fact, supported—British efforts to negotiate with Sharif Hussein, the wishes of the people of the Middle East played little role in the French/British plans to divide their land.

France was particularly interested in gaining control of the territory they dubbed "Syria," although their notions of what constituted Syria were far greater than the Syrian boundaries we identify today. In addition to modern Syria, the French demanded the territories that now constitute Lebanon, Israel, and Jordan, claiming that these all historically formed part of the greater Syrian terrain. The British claimed Mesopotamia (the region we now identify as Iraq) for direct control, and further claimed a vast territory stretching from northern Persia (Iran) to Egypt as territory that would be an independent "Arab state" subject to British influence. Thus, the Arab territory promised to Sharif Hussein was instead divided up by arbitrary borders into a cluster of states placed under either French or British control.

One territory was kept separate from French and British direct or indirect control in the Sykes-Picot negotiations. This was the region of Palestine, containing much of contemporary Israel and Jordan, and it had been designated as an "international sphere of influence," although Britain had retained the right to control the port of Haifa in its center.

In the end, the Ottoman Empire was essentially divided into British- and French-administered areas. The map Sykes and Picot produced when their meetings concluded in May 1916 showed a Middle East marked with blues and reds, the blue areas showing where France would maintain direct or indirect control and the red marking British-administered territory. Palestine—a small, brown mark in the map—was denoted as a zone of international administration.

But all of these agreements were merely setting the stage for further discord and disagreement. Sharif Hussein, believing Britain supported his claims to rule over a vast kingdom, had dispatched his son Faisal to help launch the Arab Revolt on June 6, 1916. Soon his campaign would be joined by T.E. Lawrence, dubbed "Lawrence of Arabia," who viewed with approval the network Faisal was assembling. "The bigness of the Revolt impresses me," Lawrence wrote, and described the Hashemite supporters as "mobile . . . reckless . . . impossible to make an organised force out of them." But working together, Lawrence and Faisal did make an organized force from the loose alliance, turning the Arab revolt into a headline-grabbing campaign in the conflict that became World War I. While Abdullah was responsible for much of the initial contact with the British, it was his brother Faisal who was now reaping the glory, spurring on the Arab Revolt and winning fame with Lawrence of Arabia at his side.

In 1917, Britain further altered the landscape of the Middle East through a single letter from British Foreign Secretary Arthur Balfour to a prominent British Zionist (who supported the idea of the creation of a Jewish state). This letter, which became known as the Balfour Declaration, formally stated that the British government would support the creation of a Jewish state in Palestine:

> His Majesty's Government view with favour the establishment in Palestine of a national home for the Jewish people, and will use their best endeavours to facilitate the achievement of this object, it being clearly understood that nothing

shall be done which may prejudice the civil and religious rights of existing non-Jewish communities in Palestine, or the rights and political status enjoyed by Jews in any other country.

Why did Britain make this promise? Looking forward to the war's end, British leaders viewed the territories Britain would hold in Africa and Asia and planned a land road, linking Egypt to India. With France in control of Syria and Lebanon, Britain needed a friendly presence in Palestine to protect its territories. Palestine offered protection for the British-held Suez Canal, plus opportunities for rail, pipeline, and eventually air connections between the British-dominated Gulf and the British-dominated Mediterranean.

Sharif Hussein was understandably outraged when he learned of the Balfour Declaration, believing that Palestine comprised part of the territory that had been promised to him for his "kingdom of Arabs." But British representatives appeased Hussein with a promise that Jewish settlement in Palestine would not be allowed to infringe upon "the political and economic freedom of the Arab people," a promise that would resonate decades later.

Well before the Ottoman Empire had signed an armistice, its lands had been carved up. As the Hashemites launched a revolt that, they believed, would win them a kingdom, the land they intended to claim had already been spoken for, and borders had been sketched out that would alter the politics and people of the region long after British and French claims to the region had faded away.

POSTWAR OCCUPATION

After World War I had ended with the defeat of the Ottoman armies, Britain and France set about formalizing by occupation the agreements they had drafted during the war. The Hashemite forces led by Faisal seized control of a territory stretching out from Damascus in Syria that included Jordan. But this Arab kingdom in Syria would prove short-lived.

Sharif Hussein believed that the time had come for the British to honor the promises made to him. He had supported British war efforts; his son, Faisal, had helped the British defeat the Turks. He was now ready to claim his Arab kingdom—a kingdom that would include Arabia, Syria, Lebanon, Palestine, and Iraq. He would govern from the Hijaz in Arabia; his son Faisal would remain in Damascus as King of Syria; his oldest son, Abdullah, would be named King of the Mesopotamian (Iraqi) territory and rule from Baghdad.

In 1919, Faisal traveled to London with T.E. Lawrence, where a meeting was arranged with Chaim Weizmann, a leader of the Zionist movement. They discussed the idea of a Jewish homeland to be established in Palestine, Faisal negotiating under the belief that the territory of Palestine would be part of the grand Arab kingdom. Following a second meeting in Paris, Faisal prepared the following letter:

> We feel that the Arabs and Jews are cousins in race. . . [and] have suffered similar oppression at the hands of powers stronger than themselves. . . . We Arabs, especially the educated among us, look with the deepest sympathy on the Zionist movement. . . . We will wish the Jews a hearty welcome here.

This letter provides interesting evidence of the Hashemite family's position toward the settlement of Jews in Palestine. Theirs was one of the few Arab voices expressing support for the Jewish people's wish to emigrate to the Middle East, a position that would be echoed two generations later by Abdullah's grandson, King Hussein of Jordan.

But Faisal would soon learn that the British had little intention of honoring the promises his father felt had been made. Syria had been promised to the French in the Sykes-Picot Agreement; France intended to claim its prize and did not wish to allow a British-allied ruler to remain on the throne.

British forces, unwilling to antagonize an ally, began to pull out from Syrian territory. From April 18–26, 1920, the San Remo Conference was held with the aim of finalizing the settlement of the Middle East. As a result of San Remo, France was granted mandate responsibility for Lebanon and Syria (including Faisal's kingdom), and Britain assumed responsibility for Iraq and Palestine. While the territory of Jordan was not specifically mentioned in the agreements—indication that it was viewed as unimportant by the French and British—it was assumed to be included in the territory of Palestine.

A brief resistance by Faisal's forces was quickly overcome by French forces, and the would-be "king of Syria" was forced to flee south, crossing much of the territory he and his army had seized from Ottoman hands two years earlier. Traveling south by train, under British supervision, he passed through Syria and Palestine, then on to Egypt before traveling to Europe. One witness saw him at the railway station, waiting for his train, "sitting on his luggage," while "the tears stood in his eyes and he was wounded to the soul."

HASHEMITE RULE

While Faisal's rule in Syria had been short-lived, it had given British representatives in the Middle East an idea: Rather than installing a British governor to rule over British territory, it might be more effective—and palatable to citizens of the occupied territories—to install a ruler of their own, one who would be friendly to British interests. They suggested that an Arab king might be installed in Mesopotamia (Iraq) to rule British-held territory from Baghdad.

The option became increasingly attractive as many parts of Mesopotamia erupted in riots, with demands for self-government from the people. The example of India would not work here, it was felt, and so it became a paramount concern to find the "right man" to rule Iraq.

Attention quickly turned to the Hashemite family. Abdullah was the first choice, although the reports on him were contradictory. One British intelligence officer, David Hogarth—who had never met him—relied on reports to describe Abdullah as "indolent, pleasure loving," the "least scrupulous of the brothers," "more vicious than the others," lacking a "dominant personality" and without "much will to power." He was, according to Hogarth's reports, "not born to rule." However, Hogarth stunningly concluded, "he seems the ablest" and was "regarded by Arab Intellectuals as the one cultivated member of the Family." He was "intelligent enough to grasp real facts and conform to them" and "would make a presentable titular ruler."

The fact that neither Abdullah, nor any of the Hashemite family, were natives of Mesopotamia did not to the British cause a problem for his being named king. The most important consideration was how amenable he would be to British dictates and Western influences. Gertrude Bell wrote, "Abdullah is a gentleman who likes a copy of the *Figaro* [a French newspaper] every morning at breakfast time. I haven't any doubt we should get on with him famously."

Meanwhile, Britain was under pressure to withdraw its troops from the Middle East. The war had ended; the expense of maintaining a huge military presence in the region was unpopular. Colonial Secretary Winston Churchill determined to help ease the burden on the public of maintaining expensive military forces in Mesopotamia and Palestine. He decided to establish an Arab government in Mesopotamia.

In 1921, Churchill convened a meeting in Cairo of the British experts on the Middle East region, gathering together the best minds to determine the fate of the people in the Middle East currently living under British occupation. Among those in attendance was T.E. Lawrence, who believed that if only one member of the Hashemite family was to be given a kingdom, it should be his comrade-in-arms Faisal. Faisal, Lawrence argued, had already proved his ability to rule (his short-lived kingdom in Syria); he also had proven military expertise and a commanding presence.

Faisal, when approached with the proposal of becoming king of Iraq—a kingdom already promised to his brother—insisted that Abdullah must give his approval before he would accept. Faisal then suggested that Abdullah's approval might most easily be won if Abdullah himself were promised a kingdom of his own—perhaps in the territory of Palestine.

Abdullah was not fighting for the kingdom he had been promised in Iraq, but had instead spent much of the war and postwar years fighting to retain and expand his father's control of territory in Arabia. The forces of Ibn Saud had been continually battling the Hashemites for control of the peninsula, and in May 1919, Abdullah suffered a humiliating defeat at their hands, being forced to flee across the desert in his pajamas following a surprise attack. With this attack—the Battle of Turaba—the Saudis gained critical control of Arabia in a campaign that would gradually lead to their becoming the ruling power of the entire peninsula. The British had hedged their bets by backing both the Hashemites and Saudis, offering them weapons and financing, but now they were forced to deal with a defeated Abdullah, who was leading the remains of his army north from Mecca.

Abdullah soon made contact with various Syrian exiles who had fled French-held Syria, informing them that he was leading an army to attack Damascus and re-claim Syria for the Hashemites. This was disastrous news for the British. They could not allow a British-armed-and-financed military force to attack French territory. Abdullah—accompanied by 30 officers and 200 Bedouins—reached Amman, a tiny settlement of some 2,000 people in the British-controlled territory of Palestine, in March 1921, just as Churchill's Cairo meeting was underway.

Faisal's suggestion, and the threat of an attack on French territory from British territory by a military force led by a British ally, presented a crisis to those gathered. The delegates had been leaning toward the idea of Faisal as the new king of Iraq (as Mesopotamia was now being called), believing that the riots and unrest would require a strong military presence, one that Faisal was better equipped to provide. Churchill believed that appointing Faisal king of Iraq would give the British leverage over all of the Hashemite family.

But what of Abdullah, threatening an attack on Syria from Amman in Palestine? Something must be done for him, to ensure that he supported his brother's claim to the throne in Iraq.

Finally, Winston Churchill and his colleagues in Cairo arrived at a solution. They would not give Abdullah the right to rule over all of Palestine—it was too important strategically and the British had already offered their support to a Zionist settlement there. Instead they would give him a kingdom—a kingdom precisely at the location where his army was currently camped, in the sands to the east of the Jordan river, stretching only as far as the western border of Iraq. Abdullah would be proclaimed emir of a land to be known as "Transjordan," a seemingly worthless stretch of desert with no cities or towns, no obvious resources, and a population of only 200,000, most of them expatriates and nomads.

Abdullah was given this tiny, barren kingdom, carved from Palestine, on probation. He had six months to win the support of his subjects for his rule, while avoiding any international conflicts (keeping him from attacking Syria). If he failed, he must hand his kingdom back to the British.

Abdullah accepted this arrangement reluctantly, believing that he might eventually win a better kingdom—either in Palestine or Syria. And it was with this makeshift agreement

In October 1916, T.E. Lawrence was a British intelligence officer who was sent out from Cairo to the region known as Arabia. A revolt was taking place. Arab armies had been formed and were fighting against the Ottoman armies. Following a 100-mile journey under the heat of the Arabian sun, Lawrence found the Arab leader that he thought could best lead the Arab revolt: Faisal Hussein. Working together, Faisal and Lawrence made an organized force from a loose alliance. Here, Lawrence's Arab guerrillas ride camels in the Middle Eastern desert in January 1917.

that the kingdom of Transjordan was created—as a way to keep one brother out of trouble while another brother assumed a (in British eyes) far more important role in Iraq. There was no specific economic or geographic reason for the creation of its borders; its ruler was a man who had no connection to the

A Kingdom Carved From the Desert

land—he had, in fact, simply been passing through. Its ruler had no official residence, nor was there even a capital city from which he would govern. Abdullah, the emir of Transjordan, was living in a tent—and he would remain in a tent or as a guest of friends for the first years of his reign, traveling from the small villages of Amman to Salt to Ajlun, seeking a capital and seeking support for his rule. He was dependent on the British for income, for military support, for political advice.

But Abdullah would take these humble beginnings and carve a kingdom from the wilderness. The Hashemite rule in Arabia and Iraq would vanish, but the kingdom built in Transjordan would survive.

CHAPTER

3

A Trial Kingdom

The Transjordan that was to form Abdullah I's kingdom was rife with tribal conflict by the time he was granted the right to rule it. A British officer serving in the region, C.D. Bruton, reported to his superiors that the country was close to anarchy:

> The people here do not form a homogeneous political entity. There is a sharp line of division between the settled population and the Bedouin. The former wish settled government and protection from the extortions and violence of the latter. The Bedouin prefer anarchy to order as they live from extortions from the peasantry and rapine [forcibly seizing property] as well as from their flocks and herds. You cannot expect them to form a government for their common country.

The tribal divisions in Transjordan were strong, and as Bruton had noted, marked a rough division of the population into *bedouin*—the nomad desert-dwellers—and *fellaheen*—those from a settled farming tradition. Having been largely ignored by their Ottoman rulers, having slipped through the cracks in the initial postwar occupation, the residents of Transjordan felt loyalty only to the authority of their tribal leaders, or sheikhs. For generations they had lived on tribal lands, and the shared history and culture meant far more to them than the wishes of a foreign leader or the will of a foreign power.

The challenge Abdullah faced was a large one, and the actual role that British officials felt he would ultimately play was much smaller. Concerned by the unrest in the region, and unwilling to commit a large military presence there, the British believed that Abdullah might help restore order to Transjordan, preparing it for the transition to a local person who would serve as governor. For many, including Britain's Prime Minister David Lloyd George, this vision of Transjordan was of an "Arab province or adjunct of Palestine." Abdullah was not overly powerful, nor was he a native of the region. He was, in fact, dependent on Britain, and so was an ideal choice—in British eyes—for the temporary ruler of this land bordering British-controlled territory in Palestine and Iraq.

Winston Churchill, as colonial secretary, had another plan in mind. Unrest and violence was building in Palestine between the Jewish settlers and Arabs in the region. Churchill had begun to consider a new option—the creation of two territories from Palestine: one for the Jewish or Zionist settlers, and another for the Arabs. Should it be necessary to put this plan into force, Transjordan could become the territory designated for Arabs.

This plan ignored the fact that, at the time Churchill was forming his plan, some 90 percent of the population of Palestine was not Jewish. The British used the phrase "Arabs" as a catchall; it did not reflect the vast differences separating one tribal group from another, one people with a shared history

Abdullah Ibn Hussein (1882–1951), Emir of Transjordan, during a visit to London shortly after becoming emir. In May 1946, Transjordan was granted its independence from Great Britain, and Abdullah was crowned king. Britain was allowed to station its troops in the new Hashemite Kingdom of Jordan, however, for the next 25 years.

and culture from another, nor did it acknowledge the varied beliefs of Muslims from different ethnic backgrounds. Thus, the British were able to select a family from Arabia and grant two of its members the right to rule Iraq and Transjordan. The same ignorance dictated the evolving policy toward Palestine, a policy that would permanently alter life in Transjordan and resonate for decades in the region.

The British attempts to instill order in Palestine were doomed almost from the start. The region had three official languages (Arabic, Hebrew, and English) and three holidays each week: Friday for the Muslims, Saturday for the Jews, and Sunday for the Christians. Britain had seized control of the region principally for strategic reasons—to prevent any other power from occupying it and thereby threatening Britain's valuable Suez Canal.

While Britain had agreed to allow Jewish settlement in the region, one area was exempt from this: all the territory lying between the Jordan River and the eastern boundary of Palestine. It is one of the strange twists of the fate of Palestine that the largest, least populated part of Palestine—the lands actually in need of development—were, in fact, excluded from Jewish settlement. Author John Keay notes, "To disinterested parties it seemed perverse. If anywhere could be called a 'land without a people' awaiting a 'people without land,' it was not little (cis-Jordanian) Palestine (with a population of 750,000) but this large and unfrequented (Palestinian) trans-Jordania (with a mere 220,000). Here lay the desert which might be made to bloom, here the unwanted acres whose progressive settlement need antagonize no one."

But Transjordan was disregarded as a potential venue for Jewish settlement, and the League of Nations specifically granted Britain the right to dispose of the region as it wished in its Palestine mandate of 1922. Even Abdullah seemed to have initially disregarded the land he had been given, viewing it as merely a stopping point on his way to Syria. In fact, Abdullah's closest advisors at the beginning of his tenure were, for the most part, Syrians who had been forced out or fled when France took possession of Syria. They were mostly anti-French, anti-Zionist, upper-class city dwellers who looked down upon the Transjordanians, and threatened British interests in Palestine and its desire to maintain peaceful relations with France in Syria.

The French ambassador was soon protesting Abdullah's actions in Transjordan, claiming that the choice of Hashemite rulers on two of Syria's borders (with Transjordan and Iraq) was threatening the stability of French governance in Syria. Initially, the British argued that in fact their choice of Abdullah had been designed for precisely the opposite reason—to protect Syria from Hashemite attacks—but when the French governor of Syria, Henri Gouraud, was the target of an assassination attempt, suspicion was soon directed at Abdullah and his allies, particularly when the four suspected assassins were proved to be living openly in Transjordan.

It seemed that the six-month experiment of Abdullah as ruler of Transjordan had been a failure. He had failed to curtail his ambitions to spark unrest in Syria; the funds being provided to him by Britain were being handed out to his friends and family members; and he had done little to build a stable government in Transjordan. The people viewed Abdullah's Syrian allies as wasteful and incompetent, and their would-be ruler as weak and unpopular. He had, in fact, even failed to establish a permanent capital—or a permanent home for himself. Abdullah, it seemed, was ill suited to govern the land he distastefully described as "this wilderness."

END OF AN EXPERIMENT

As the six months of his temporary governance of Transjordan neared an end, British officials were nearly unanimous in viewing the experiment as a failure. Nearly unanimous, but with one important exception—T.E. Lawrence, who in 1922 was sent out to Transjordan by Winston Churchill to make an

T.E. Lawrence (Lawrence of Arabia, left) and Lowell Thomas (right) at Lawrence's headquarters near Acava, in Arabia. Lawrence, considered an expert on Arab affairs, was dispatched by Winston Churchill to assess the situation under Abdullah in Jordan. Lawrence, a staunch supporter of the Arab people, was probably the only reason Abdullah was allowed to remain in power. Thomas traveled with Lawrence and brought his famed exploits to the world.

assessment of Abdullah's control and, in essence, to take steps to return Transjordan to British control.

Lawrence believed that Abdullah should remain in power, however. Using an argument that he knew would appeal to Churchill, with his focus on the financial cost of foreign efforts, Lawrence astutely reported, "His total cost is less than a battalion; his regime prejudices us in no way, whatever eventual solution we wish to carry out, provided that it is not too popular and not too efficient."

Lawrence knew that the British leadership was still internally debating the fate of Palestine—whether it should be permanently divided into two separate entities, with Transjordan becoming the "Arab" state; whether Abdullah's father, Sharif Hussein, should be allowed to claim Palestine for part of his kingdom in the Hijaz. As these matters were still undecided, it was not necessarily a bad plan to allow Abdullah to continue his "temporary" rule over Transjordan.

The British intelligence officer H. St. John Philby was soon dispatched as an advisor to Abdullah. Philby busily began laying the framework for self-government in Transjordan, while other British representatives began to shape from the Bedouin forces a more disciplined army under British command. Soon, the chaos began to evaporate and law and order began to create a more livable environment in the region.

Abdullah embraced the changes the British had foisted upon him, and slowly began to warm to the land that he had been given. By 1922, his British subsidy had been increased, and a year later, he had received the first written recognition of "an independent government in Trans-Jordan under His Highness the Amir Abdullah ibn Husayn," the first official acknowledgement of himself as king. As with every British agreement negotiated with Abdullah, however, there were strings attached. Abdullah was charged with establishing a constitutional government, and establishing what the British rather openly described as "a satisfactory" agreement between the two countries.

Abdullah was still very much dependent on British support for his reign—and for his country's existence. In 1922, the Hashemite's enemy in Arabia, Ibn Saud, led a force into the southeast of Transjordan to attack Abdullah. The force, several thousand strong, came within an hour's camel ride of Transjordan's town of Amman before British planes and armored cars forced them to retreat.

An even greater threat came two years later, from Abdullah's own father, Sharif Hussein. In early 1924, the elderly sharif arrived in Amman, accompanied by three trains hauling troops for laying railroads tracks and several railroad cars. Their aim was to complete a railway line leading from Medina (in Arabia) to Amman.

The British were concerned by the arrival of the sharif. They knew that he had been unhappy with his son for his willingness to take orders from the British, rather than from his kingdom in Hijaz. Portions of Transjordan had once been part of the sharif's territory; they believed that the opening of the railway might lead him to reclaim this, plus all of the land currently under his son's rather weak control.

The father quickly made himself comfortable in Amman and showed no signs of leaving, as construction of the rail lines began. Within a few weeks, as word reached Amman that the last Ottoman caliph—designated the spiritual leader of all Muslims—had been deposed in Turkey, Sharif Hussein proclaimed himself the new caliph.

The British government had been paying subsidies to all three Hashemite leaders, and had no intention of allowing the sharif to disrupt the region's politics—or attempt to dictate religious policy for the nation whose empire contained the largest percentage of all Muslims in the world—namely, Britain. Sharif Hussein was quickly reminded that in exchange for his cash payments, he would need to endorse the British mandate of Palestine (thus agreeing to support Zionist settlement there) and sign a peace treaty with Ibn Saud. If he refused, and his son supported him in this refusal, Sharif Hussein and Abdullah could leave Transjordan at once.

Hussein eventually agreed, returning to the Hijaz. Only four months later, Ibn Saud again attacked Sharif Hussein's territory, capturing the holy city of Mecca in October. Hussein was forced to abdicate, and his kingdom vanished into what would become Saudi Arabia.

Bowing to British demands, Transjordan soon became one of the few oases of stability in the region. There were revolts in

Egypt; Palestine was becoming a battleground between Zionist settlers and Palestinians; in French-held Syria fighting was underway in the streets of Damascus. In Transjordan, though, Abdullah had finally settled in Amman, and under direct British management, his nation was becoming a model of efficiency and effective colonial oversight.

FOREIGN INFLUENCES

Under British direction, a new government began to take shape in Transjordan. Since the ruler himself was an outsider, it is not surprising that so many of those assuming positions in the emerging government were foreign, as well. Britain controlled the finances, and British officials worked behind the scenes, directing policy, but even at lower levels of the civil service, recruitment focused on non-natives, as it was felt that Transjordan lacked the kind of educated and experienced men necessary to shape a new government.

On February 20, 1928, an agreement was signed between Britain and Abdullah, formalizing the relationship between the two. It was an unequal relationship, spelled out in the clauses that cited the conditional and subordinate nature of any and all local powers to British authority. In the agreement, Abdullah agreed to be "guided by the advice" or "refer for the advice" of British authorities; it was, however, reassuring to Abdullah in that it recognized the existence of a government "under the rule of His Highness the Amir of Transjordan."

That same year, Transjordan took a significant step to formalize its attempts at self-government, albeit under British direction. In April 1928, an Organic Law—or constitution—was drafted, announcing the creation of a 21-member Legislative Council, each member serving a three-year term. There were checks to this council, however: The emir appointed one-third of its members, and his chief minister served as the council's chair, the only member able to introduce bills for discussion or debate. In addition, the council would meet only three months of the year, and it could be dissolved by the emir at any time.

As systems began to stabilize the situation in Transjordan, Abdullah once more turned his eyes to other territory. As it seemed less and less likely that he would be able to acquire the throne in Syria, he turned instead to another territory: Palestine. Despite British discouragement of his ambitions, Abdullah continually proposed to the British the idea of uniting Transjordan and Palestine under a single king—that king being, of course, Abdullah.

As Transjordan had grown more stable, an increasing number of Palestinians had moved to the neighboring territory. Many of these were merchants, eager to take advantage of a new market for their goods and trade. A smaller number were refugees, fleeing the violence that was occurring on the streets of Jerusalem and other parts of the territory.

Palestinian activists, fighting against Zionist settlement in their lands, had little love for Abdullah. They viewed him as a traitor to the Arab cause, collaborating with the British simply to retain his kingdom. Abdullah had also maintained a limited cooperation with Jewish authorities in Palestine, in large part because a complete overthrow of British control in Palestine might lead to revolution, spreading eastward to Transjordan. This benign cooperation, of course, further inflamed Palestinian activists against Abdullah.

Abdullah retained his dream of ruling over a larger Arab state in the region, and no doubt he hoped to win Jewish support for the idea of a partitioned Palestine as a sensible solution to the increasing violence. By 1937, the British were giving serious consideration to the idea. The Zionists firmly supported the partitioning of Palestine—an important evolution from the idea of a Jewish "homeland" to the creation of an actual, separate, Jewish state.

The British Royal Commission envisioned an Arab state that would consist of Transjordan plus what was described as "the Arab part of Palestine"—in order words, those areas of Palestine that did not include the Jewish state, areas of strategic importance (such as Haifa), and areas of religious importance (Jerusalem).

Problems remained, however. No matter how the boundaries of a Jewish state were drafted, the area would still contain as many Arabs as Jews, necessitating the forced emigration of Arabs elsewhere—most likely to Transjordan. This would create such problems that the British eventually abandoned the idea of partition.

WAR AND PEACE

By the time of World War II, Abdullah was firmly established in Transjordan. He had been its ruler for some 18 years. He had demonstrated an ability to maintain order in an increasingly unstable region of the world. Transjordan provided an important base for the British during the war, and much of the Transjordan-based Arab Legion performed heroically in service to Britain. As part of the war effort, Britain financed the development of the port city of Aqaba on the Red Sea.

Abdullah's loyalty was rewarded in May 1946, following the signing of a new Anglo-Transjordanian treaty that formally brought an end to the mandate and announced the creation of an independent state. Abdullah was crowned king of the Hashemite Kingdom of Transjordan. Twenty-five years after arriving in the land, Abdullah had successfully established a kingdom for the Hashemites.

The independence of this new entity was not total, however. Britain retained the right to base its troops there for 25 years. Britain would continue to pay a subsidy to the kingdom, and British officers would continue to command the Jordanian army. The tiny kingdom, with its population of less than half a million, had few other friends. The Syrians and Iraqis (no longer led by Abdullah's brother, who had died several years earlier) were suspicious of Abdullah's ambitions. The Saudis still viewed him as an enemy and believed that Transjordan contained territory that should have belonged to them. The Palestinians were suspicious of Abdullah's efforts to negotiate with the Zionists. The Egyptians viewed him as a British puppet. The Soviets vetoed Transjordan's nomination for membership in the United Nations. The United States refused to recognize the new kingdom, influenced in part by Jewish opposition to any separation of Palestine's mandated territory.

Events in postwar Transjordan were dramatically impacted by the situation in Palestine. Unrest had grown so great that Britain, unable to maintain order, had turned instead to the United Nations. Debates focused the idea of partitioning Palestine into two distinct "Jewish" and "Arab" states.

Although the British could not openly favor partition, in February 1948, they met with Abdullah behind the scenes, under guise of renegotiating the Anglo-Transjordanian treaty, and gave him to understand that they would certainly not interfere with any moves that might involve the use of Jordan's military force in Palestine, as long as it did not interfere with the area reserved for the Jewish state.

The United Nations gradually came to a conclusion: slightly more than 55 percent of Palestine was granted to Jewish settlers to form a Jewish state—resulting in a situation where more than half of the territory was given to less than 30 percent of the population. Hundreds of thousands of Arabs would find themselves on the Jewish side of the divided territory when Britain evacuated on May 14, 1948.

The city of Jerusalem was granted a special status. Because of its religious significance to Islam, Judaism, and Christianity, it would not be placed on either side of the dividing line but instead would be placed under international jurisdiction.

On May 14, 1948, the new state of Israel was officially proclaimed. Within 24 hours it was under attack, as armies from Egypt, Iraq, Lebanon, Syria, and Transjordan invaded its borders.

After the partitioning of Palestine in 1948, many families found themselves to be homeless refugees. This Palestinian family camped out in the ruins of the Roman amphitheater in Amman.

King Abdullah was at the forefront of the Transjordanian army. Only hours after the state of Israel had officially been proclaimed, he and his staff stood at the east end of the Allenby bridge, which spanned the Jordan River and joined with the main road into Jerusalem. The border was unguarded; British military had evacuated hours earlier. Britain's representative in Amman, Alec Kirkbride, witnessed the scene:

> At twelve o'clock precisely the King drew his revolver, fired a symbolical shot into the air and shouted the word "forward." The long column of Jordanian troops, which stretched down the road behind the bridge, already had the engines of their cars ticking over and, as they moved off at the word of command, the hum of their motors rose to a roar.

As Abdullah led a force across the bridge, others of his troops invaded Samaria from the north. He commanded a force of around 6,000 to 7,000 men, approximately one-third of the invading Arab force, and although his troops were smaller in number than the large contingent sent by Egypt, they were well organized and experienced. As Jewish forces moved into Jerusalem, Abdullah eventually dispatched his own Arab Legion to the international zone. He knew that an attempt to capture the prize city would bring international censure, but he felt an historic obligation to try. Abdullah, like all the Hashemites, traced his family back to the prophet Muhammad and knew the religious significance of overseeing the holy city.

The fighting in and around Jerusalem was intense, and Abdullah's forces suffered heavy casualties. The United Nations had launched an arms embargo against all fighting sides in the conflict, and Britain honored the ban. Refugees began pouring across the border into Transjordan, fleeing the fighting. By June 1948, about 300,000 Palestinians had fled their homes, many of them crossing into Transjordan. In July, Jewish forces seized the towns of Lydda and Ramle, following Arab withdrawal from the region. Most of the Arab population was forced from their homes, and long columns of refugees began the journey east to Transjordan.

Abdullah wished to maintain his position, hold onto the gained territory, and ensure that the refugees pouring into Transjordan did not create a domestic crisis. A year earlier, a constitutional amendment had referred to the Hashemite kingdom as "Jordan" rather than "Transjordan," and rather than being an error, this was a sign that Abdullah intended a kingdom that encompassed both sides of the River Jordan, not only its east bank but its west bank as well.

Several truces were signed and then broken. Finally, Transjordan signed an armistice agreement with Israel on April 3, 1949. Israel had gained an additional 5,180 square kilometers of territory originally intended to form part of the

Arab state—in Galilee, the Negev Desert, and the area around Jerusalem. In exchange, Transjordan gained 5,880 square kilometers in eastern Palestine (also known as the West Bank) and East Jerusalem.

The region was soon dotted with borders—and points of conflict. The city of Jerusalem was divided between Israeli and Jordanian territory. Refugees streamed into Transjordan. About 800,000 Palestinians fled their homes, many of them the wealthy and well educated. The land once intended for an Arab state was divided.

Abdullah remained intent on annexing the territory occupied by Transjordan and uniting it with his kingdom. He wanted to ensure that the move came not as a hostile takeover, however, but instead at the request of the Palestinian people in the occupied territory. He offered Jordanian citizenship to all West Bank Arabs, and removed restrictions on travel and customs when crossing the Jordan River. He replaced the military administration in the West Bank with a civilian one, and then named three Palestinian ministers to his cabinet.

Finally, in April 1950, elections were held for a new, 40-member Chamber of Deputies, with an equal number of seats designated for representatives from the East and West Bank. Similarly, in the appointed members of the Senate, an equal number of seats were designated for the East and West Bank representatives. The move was loudly trumpeted as a sign of equality, but it is important to note that the representation from the East and West Banks was not proportional. The population of the West Bank was nearly twice that of the East Bank, beginning a tradition of bias and conflict between Jordanian-born and Palestinian-born residents that would resonate into the reign of King Abdullah II, more than 50 years later. It is also important to note that Chamber members elected from the West Bank were largely educated, urban professionals, quite different from the East Bank representatives—twelve landowners, five professionals (two civil servants), and two merchants.

On April 25, 1950, several of the Palestinian representatives in the Jordanian parliament proposed a motion to unify the West and East Banks, a motion that was passed unanimously. Abdullah had achieved at least part of his aim. His original kingdom still formed 94 percent of the new, unified nation, but only one-third of its population. The East Bank was largely undeveloped, its population undereducated, and its industries nonexistent. The population of the West Bank was wealthier and better educated, and its economy more advanced.

Abdullah would rule over this expanded kingdom for less than a year and a half, however. On July 20, 1951, while he was attending the al-Aqsa Mosque in Jerusalem for Friday prayers, following a visit to the grave of his father, Sharif Hussein, King Abdullah was shot by a Palestinian gunman. He was 69 years old. At his side was his 16-year-old grandson, Hussein, who narrowly missed being shot himself as guards from his grandfather's security force wildly fired in an effort to kill the assassin.

Abdullah was the victim of both his efforts to seize Palestinian territory and of his pro-British negotiations. Within 16 years, the territory Abdullah had added to Transjordan would be lost. But he left behind a kingdom that would stand, a kingdom that had been carved from unwanted land in the desert.

CHAPTER

4

Early Years in an Unstable Time

King Abdullah II's coronation followed intense debates and arguments over the rights of succession, and his father's ascension to the throne was no different. The same principles that governed King Hussein's decision initially governed the right of succession after King Abdullah I's assassination. The king had had three wives and fathered two sons, Talal and Nayif.

Talal, born in 1909 to King Abdullah's first wife, was the oldest son. He attended school at the Royal Military Academy Sandhurst, in Britain, but he had spent little time with his father. When he returned from school in England in 1927, he was given some makeshift work in the kingdom's government. He married his cousin, Zein, and his first child, a son named Hussein, was born in 1935. Disagreements and tension with his father grew as the frustrated Talal looked for a role that fit in the kingdom. Sadly, at this

Early Years in an Unstable Time

King Talal of Jordan (right), eldest son of King Abdullah and his first wife, took the throne in 1951 shortly after Abdullah was struck, at age 69, by a Palestinian assassin's bullet. Talal reigned less than a year; he was found incompetent because of increasingly severe bouts of schizophrenia and was removed from power. His son, Hussein, assumed power, with Hussein's mother serving as regent until Hussein was of age.

same time he began to show signs of mental illness, resulting in an eventual diagnosis of schizophrenia.

With Talal's behavior becoming increasingly erratic, involving alcoholism, violent acts, and outspoken criticism of the British, Abdullah turned to his younger son, Talal's half-brother Nayif. Nayif was five years younger than Talal, with an unexceptional—although unobjectionable—personality. It soon became clear that the king favored a succession in which

Nayif would serve as regent, ruling the kingdom until Abdullah's favorite grandson, Hussein, would be old enough to assume the throne.

When Abdullah was assassinated, Talal was in Switzerland receiving medical treatment. Nayif was named the regent. For seven weeks, the kingdom was rocked by chaos. Anti-Palestinian riots broke out in Amman, Abdullah's bodyguards violently lashed out in Jerusalem, and other Arab leaders eyed with interest the political vacuum in Jordan.

Meanwhile, Nayif had little interest in a temporary stewardship of Jordan—serving only until his nephew was ready to become king. He made it clear that he expected to be named king himself, and would not confirm the death sentences of those found guilty of his father's murder unless his wish was granted. He even threatened to resign, throwing an already chaotic kingdom open to political confusion or even invasion.

At this point, contact was made with Talal in Switzerland, and news quickly traveled back that Talal seemed quite sane. Nayif threatened a military coup, but the British still in Jordan made it clear that an orderly succession was critical to maintaining Jordan's stability and that Talal was now the man to do it. He returned from Switzerland in September, and immediately assumed the throne.

King's Talal's coronation restored stability to the streets of Jordan, and his reign began optimistically. He was popular among his people, and he had a strong and determined wife and three sons, the oldest of whom had already been designated as crown prince.

He was liberal, and launched a campaign to reform the British-influenced Constitution of 1946. The Constitution of 1952 that emerged did guarantee more personal freedoms, but it still ensured that the executive branch retained control over the legislature. The constitution was officially adopted on New Year's Day, and it remains Talal's crowning achievement. There would be few others to mark his reign.

By the spring of 1952, Talal's behavior had again become erratic and violent. He refused to seek treatment. Once more rumors of instability were fanned by interested parties, including the king's half-brother Nayif, and other Arab leaders, particularly the Hashemite ruler in Iraq. Talal was persuaded to take a vacation to Europe, and a Throne Council was formed by the cabinet to exercise the king's powers. The king's hospitalization was requested, but Talal stubbornly refused arguments from his advisors and family members.

In August, a rebellion of military officers in Egypt overthrew the monarchy there. Fearful that Talal's weakness and instability would spark a similar revolt in Jordan, the parliament convened and took the historic step, on August 11, 1952, of unanimously voting for the king to be forced to abdicate because of insanity.

Sixteen-year-old Crown Prince Hussein was in Switzerland, on a vacation break from his British school Harrow, outside London, when he learned of the dramatic events. He later remembered how his new role was announced to him: "There was a knock on the door, and the hotel page delivered a cablegram from the Royal Court in Jordan, addressed to 'His Majesty, King Hussein'."

The new monarch finished his studies at Harrow, and completed a condensed course at the British Royal Military Academy at Sandhurst to receive his commission, before returning to rule Jordan. He ascended to the throne at the age of 18, beginning a reign that would last nearly 47 years.

THE NEW KING

The kingdom Hussein had inherited posed numerous challenges, many of them the result of the conflict in Palestine. The population of Jordan had tripled, with one-third of the total new population consisting of 458,000 Palestinian refugees. Jordan faced tremendous challenges in simply administering the new refugees and the refugee camps they required.

Prince Hussein of Jordan, at age 16. In this 1951 photo, he poses in a fencing costume given to him by his grandfather as a reward for winning a medal at Victoria College, in Egypt. Hussein accompanied his grandfather, King Abdullah I, the day he was assassinated outside a Jerusalem mosque.

They were mostly illiterate and poor, and their camps were closely supervised by Jordanian police, leading to lasting charges of discrimination that would continue to trouble Jordan when Abdullah II became king. It was a classic clash of cultures between the urban Palestinians and the rural Jordanians.

In addition, although the Palestinians had sought refuge in Jordan, they viewed the country—much as Abdullah had when he first claimed the territory—as merely a temporary stop. They wanted to return to their homeland, and wanted a host government that would do everything in its power to ensure that this return was expedited. Many were dissatisfied with the stance of the Hashemites: their willingness to negotiate and their pro-Western point of view. Many favored instead a more activist, pro-Arab attitude, like that demonstrated by Egypt's leader, Nasser.

In the beginning, Hussein's greatest challenge was to cement his power in the kingdom. He was caught in the crossfire not only between native Jordanians and Palestinian refugees, but also—as the Cold War unfolded—between the Soviets and their allies (neighboring Egypt, Syria, and Saudi Arabia) and pro-Western pressure from Britain and others (including neighboring Iraq, Turkey, and Iran).

Hussein was ideally suited to navigate these complex and often conflicting demands. He was comfortable with both Arab and Western groups, and had lived both in Jordan's bustling but underdeveloped capital and in more cosmopolitan cities of Europe. He was, in the beginning, however, hampered by his youth and inexperience. He wavered between shaping his government with young and more liberal leaders and with those older, more experienced politicians who were tainted by their connections to old regimes controlled by the British. This zigzagging resulted in the rapid arrival and departure of prime ministers—during one nine-month period, five prime ministers were appointed and then dismissed. The longest lasting government survived for only nine months.

The climate began to shift with the British-French-Israeli invasion of Egypt in 1956, known as the Suez Crisis. Pro-Egypt and anti-British sentiment was strong in Jordan, and King Hussein was determined to bow to the trend. The Anglo-Jordanian Treaty of 1948 was eventually terminated. Financial support to the kingdom was instead offered by Egypt, Saudi Arabia, and Syria, although only Saudi Arabia actually delivered on any promises of payment. The change marked a shift in Jordanian policy, away from the West and more in alliance with Arab nations.

A MILITARY CHALLENGE

Some historians suggest that the most critical period in the reign of the Hashemites occurred in April 1957, when King Hussein faced the threat of a military coup. Military officers, some loyal to General Nasser in Egypt and eager to exploit confusion in the regime to seize power, attempted to launch a coup. On the night of April 13, Hussein learned that fighting had broken out in an army base in Zarqa, and he immediately went there, only to discover troops battling each other. Hussein quickly broke into the middle of the fighting, rallied his loyalists, and brought an end to the revolt.

The rapid conclusion to the revolt demonstrated Hussein's courage and resolve, ensuring that the revolution in Egypt did not spread to Jordan. The monarch in Iraq would not be so lucky; Hussein's cousin there, little more than a year later, would be swiftly overwhelmed by the military and executed as the officers seized power.

Hussein responded to the crisis by cementing his control over military appointments, loading his army with the Bedouins who had proved most loyal to his regime. On April 25, 1957, he declared martial law. He took action to suppress opposition political parties and trade unions, opposition newspapers, and also exercised greater control over parliamentary elections. This was not a temporary fix—Hussein would maintain a firm control over any political activity in his kingdom for the next three decades.

As British forces prepared to depart from Jordan in July 1957, Hussein negotiated a deal with the United States for aid. This aid would help spark economic development in the country.

Construction and the creation of a modern highway system helped address Jordan's unemployment; tourism in Jerusalem, Bethlehem, and sites in the East and West Bank added to Jordan's prosperity.

BIRTH OF ABDULLAH

By the 1960s, Jordan had entered a period of relative stability and economic growth. It was during this period that Hussein's first son, Abdullah was born. Hussein married for the first time to Sharifa Dina bin Abdul Hamid, the Egyptian-born third cousin of his father, on April 19, 1955. He was 19; his bride was a 26-year-old graduate of Cambridge University and a former lecturer in English literature at Cairo University. The marriage lasted only 18 months and produced Hussein's first child, a daughter named Alia.

In 1961, Hussein married a young Englishwoman, Antoinette Gardiner, who converted to Islam and became known as Princess Muna. Princess Muna was the daughter of a British army officer. Their son, Abdullah, was born January 30, 1962. A second son, Faisal, followed one year later. Twin daughters, Aisha and Zein, were born in 1968.

Shortly after his birth, Abdullah was proclaimed crown prince, a title that had been held by his uncle, Hassan. Only a short time later, however, the issue of the Palestinians once more began to haunt the Jordanian monarchy. In 1964, Hussein had, with some hesitation, agreed to approve the creation of a separate political organization to speak for the Palestinians—a role he had previously claimed for himself. The Palestine Liberation Organization (PLO) had Hussein's reluctant approval, but little else. It was not allowed to raise funds from those Palestinians living in Jordan, nor was it allowed to train its military units in Jordan.

By the mid-1960s, Jordan's support of the PLO had ended. Allowing the PLO to be based in Jordan had proved a trigger for unrest. Suddenly, a new identity was being created on

Jordanian soil. Where once connections with Arabism and Islam, or clans and tribes, had been paramount, suddenly the label of "Palestinian" became a separate form of identity. Those living in the West Bank now embraced the identity of Palestinians, viewing their connection to Jordan as only temporary and adopting a more aggressive anti-Israel stance.

The PLO began a campaign calling on Jordanians to overthrow the king, and bombs were planted in Amman. Concerned by the threats against his life, and the potential danger to his son, Crown Prince Abdullah, Hussein decided to change the official succession and make provisions for the very real possibility that he might be assassinated. Determined to preserve Jordan's stability, even after his death, he decided that the crown should pass not to his toddler son but instead to his brother, Hassan. Abdullah's first period as crown prince had lasted little more than three years, from his birth to April 1, 1965. The title would not return to him until February 7, 1999.

EARLY EDUCATION

In 1966, the young Abdullah began his education at the Islamic Educational College, a small private school in Amman. This would be his only experience with Jordanian schools; at the age of five, he was sent to England to attend St. Edmund's School in Surrey.

St. Edmund's was founded in 1874 and located on the grounds of a 35-acre estate that was once the home of George Bernard Shaw. St. Edmund's was not as stark and austere as some English boarding schools, and it had a focus on sports that appealed to the active, athletic young Abdullah. The all-boys school boasted a number of distinguished alumni, including poet W.H. Auden and writer Christopher Isherwood, but it remained a dramatic change from the sheltered palace life Abdullah had known in Jordan. Although Abdullah was assigned a private tutor for Arabic and Islamic studies, his education during these early years was clearly influenced by the West. He would remain at St. Edmund's until the age of 13, when he traveled to the United States to enroll in Eaglebrook School.

While Abdullah was beginning his education in England, his native land was caught in a climate of increasing unrest. Border clashes with Syria and Israel continued to intensify. Israel announced plans to divert the waters of the Jordan River for irrigation, then launched an attack on the West Bank village of Samu, killing some 20 Jordanian soldiers and many more civilians. King Hussein called for a mandatory draft; war with Israel seemed inevitable.

Soon, Syria, Egypt, and Jordan had closed ranks, and troops were moved to those nations' borders with Israel. Egypt took further action when it closed the Straits of Tiran, the access route to the southern port of Eliat, to Israeli ships. Israel protested the decision to close the straits, but it did not wait for an international response.

On June 5, 1967, Israelis forces launched a surprise air attack, in a single action eliminating the Egyptian, Jordanian, and Syrian air forces before they could become airborne. Israeli forces quickly advanced across Sinai, passing the Suez Canal, and also seizing Jerusalem's Old City and occupying Gaza, Jordan's West Bank territories, and the Syrian-occupied Golan Heights. Within a single week, Israel had seized control of 100 percent of the territory once deemed Palestine, plus substantial portions of Syrian and Egyptian land. In a single week, Jordan lost the West Bank and so lost a substantial portion of its income, about half of its industrial capacity, 25 percent of its arable land, 60 percent of its fruit and vegetable production, more than one-third of its grain production and livestock, and the treasured holy sites that had generated 90 percent of Jordan's tourism revenue.

Of the devastating defeat, Hussein would later comment, "The losses were tremendous, but the fact is that we are proud that we fought honorably and we are proud of our men, proud of the fact that despite all the odds, we were able to stand Israel."

A CHASTENED RULER

The war had cost Jordan much of its income and land, but it brought another consequence: more refugees. More than 250,000 Palestinians fled into Jordan after the war, creating a Jordan whose population now contained nearly as many Palestinians as Jordanians. There were now more Palestinians in Jordan than in the land that once been known as Palestine.

Hussein had clearly seen evidence of Israel's military might. He determined to pursue a policy of negotiation, rather than antagonism, toward Jordan's neighbor to the west. This was the emergence of Hussein as diplomat, a role he would serve until his final months of life. He astutely saw that Jordan was too weak to serve as a military power in the volatile Middle East, but it could play a critical role as a source of stability in the region.

This policy sparked tremendous dissatisfaction among the Palestinians living in Jordan, and the dissatisfaction was fanned by certain wings of the PLO under the leadership of Yasser Arafat. Soon discontent was spreading throughout the Jordanian refugee camps, and refugees began banding together, with PLO prompting and with arms from Syria and financing from other Arab states. They began their own independence movement, intent on launching an attack on Israel from Jordan to reclaim the Palestinian territory.

Conflict began to build within Jordan. Hussein's motorcade was fired upon. PLO groups would arbitrarily seize the cars of wealthy passersby, or extort "protection money" from shopkeepers and merchants.

The violence escalated in September 1970, when Jordan plunged into civil war. Fearing the threat of his overthrow, Hussein ordered his military to drive out the Palestinian militias from Jordan. Syrian forces then began to move south in support of the Palestinian groups, while Israeli troops massed on the border to support Hussein. But the military fiercely drove out the Syrians, and then systematically wiped out the

Thousands of people, including armed Palestinian guerrillas, march through the center of Amman in August 1969, calling for a Holy War to exact revenge for a fire at the al-Aqsa Mosque in Jerusalem. Palestinians accused Israel of setting the blaze, although a Christian tourist, who was later judged insane and deported, admitted that he lit the fire.

Palestinian guerrilla camps, forcing the majority of them to flee to Lebanon. Although it would take several months before the government and military could successfully wipe all PLO camps out of the country, those who fled would adopt the name "Black September," the month in which Hussein first began the determined—and violent—campaign to drive the guerrillas from his country.

In 1972, Hussein and Princess Muna divorced. Only a few months later, he married Alia Toukan, the young daughter of the former Jordanian ambassador to Britain, whose family was of Palestinian heritage. It was an interesting—and perhaps politically astute—move for Hussein to choose as his third wife a woman of Palestinian heritage at a time when Palestinians comprised nearly half of Jordan's population but when biases and suspicions between Jordanians and Palestinians were high. Only months earlier, Palestinian commandos had made multiple attempts to hijack Jordanian aircraft, and the Jordanian prime minister had been assassinated by Black September activists.

Princess Alia became extraordinarily popular and beloved. In 1972, she gave birth to a daughter, Haya. Their son, Ali, was born in 1975, and the couple adopted a young Palestinian girl, Abir, in 1976, after her mother was killed in a plane crash near the Amman airport. Tragically, Princess Alia herself would be killed in a helicopter crash in Amman on February 9, 1977, after only four years of marriage.

Palestinian issues remained very much the focus of much of Hussein's efforts in the 1970s. He continued to argue over the PLO—about who had the role of speaking for the Palestinian people in diplomatic negotiations, as well as who would serve as their representative in the East Bank.

CHAPTER

5

An American Education

While his father was wrestling with Palestinian issues, and enjoying his brief marriage to Princess Alia, Abdullah had left the now-familiar surroundings of St. Edmund's School in England and traveled to the United States. Here, he was enrolled at Eaglebrook School, a small, private school for boys in grades six through nine. Located in Deerfield, Massachusetts, Eaglebrook has a 700-acre campus on Pocumtuck Mountain.

Although Eaglebrook has many distinguished alumni, and many of its students were sons of prominent families, not many were the sons of kings, nor were many from the Middle East. Abdullah continued with his private tutoring in Arabic and Islamic, although English was the language he was most comfortable speaking. The English he spoke was with a British accent, however—another novelty in the small Massachusetts school.

Abdullah chose to remain in the same region of the United States to continue his education after he had completed his studies at Eaglebrook. He next enrolled at Deerfield Academy, a prestigious prep school in the same town as Eaglebrook, where he completed his secondary education. Abdullah often returned to Jordan during school vacations, but the majority of his formative years were spent in the West.

In 1980, Abdullah chose to follow in his father's (and grandfather's) footsteps by enrolling at the prestigious Royal Military Academy Sandhurst, in Surrey, England. Many of Jordan's top military officers were trained at Sandhurst, and it is the official training location for all British army officers as well as those of other nations.

Following a six-month intensive training course, Abdullah received the commission of second lieutenant in 1981. He then took additional courses in military training, military history, and political and international affairs. He was later appointed a Reconnaissance Troop Leader in the 13th/18th Battalion of the Royal Hussars (a division of the British Army), assigned to the territories of then-West Germany and England.

AN ERA OF CHANGE

In 1978, Abdullah's father, King Hussein, took as his fourth wife American-born Lisa Halaby. The 26-year-old converted to Islam upon her marriage and became known as Queen Noor. Given that she was only ten years older than he was, Abdullah (and the older group of his siblings and half-siblings) referred to their new stepmother as *Abla Noor*, or "Big Sister Noor."

Crown Prince Hassan remained the king's official regent when Hussein was traveling or out of the country. He had performed these duties ably, demonstrated skill in dealing with the PLO, and become a champion of Jordanian education and economic reform. Most Jordanians believed that the king's brother would be the one to succeed him. Palace gossip also mentioned the king's son with Princess Alia, Prince Ali, as a

An American Education 71

King Hussein and his son, Prince Abdullah, in Amman. In this 1984 photo, they wait for Queen Elizabeth II to arrive on an official visit.

potential heir to the throne. In later years, Hussein and Queen Noor's son, Prince Hamzah, would frequently emerge as a favorite of his father's.

Sensing that the choice of Hussein's successor was uncertain, Abdullah wisely chose to concentrate on building a solid career in the military. After completing his studies at Sandhurst, Abdullah spent a year at Oxford University in England, pursuing postgraduate studies in Middle Eastern Affairs, before returning to Jordan.

In 1984, he joined the Jordanian Armed Forces as a first lieutenant. He served as platoon commander and company second-in-command in the 40th Armored Brigade, quickly establishing a reputation for hard work and skill in commanding his fellow soldiers, many of them Bedouins.

As Abdullah was focusing on Jordan's military, his father was determined to find a nonmilitary solution to conflict in the region. By the early 1980s, the PLO had been expelled from their headquarters in Lebanon by an Israeli invasion. PLO leader Arafat was weakened and became determined to work toward an easing of the tension within Jordan, and specifically the conflict with King Hussein. The two leaders met in 1983.

In March 1984, elections were held in Jordan—the first in 17 years and the first in which women could vote; political parties, however, remained outlawed.

LAND FOR PEACE

Hussein's role in the Middle East was a challenging one. Periodically marginalized by American presidents like Jimmy Carter and Ronald Reagan, who attempted to negotiate their own Middle East peace treaties without Jordanian involvement—and often without Palestinian involvement—Hussein in the 1980s proposed a formula for ending conflict known as "Land for Peace." Hussein's idea was that an Arab-Israeli peace depended upon Israel's returning the land it had seized in 1967.

Several years later, in an appearance on the American television program "NewsHour," he explained his motivation:

> Well, peace, if it comes to that part of the world, will mean a great difference to a lot of people and the areas important to the rest of the world. It will mean peace between the followers of the three great religions. It will mean an entirely new future for that entire region, and it will mean the removal of the root cause of a lot of instability within the region and beyond. So isn't that worth the effort?

Syria strongly opposed the agreement, and violent opposition from numerous sources to Hussein's efforts resulted in the assassination of Jordanian diplomats as they traveled abroad.

By 1985, Hussein had issued a statement that he would not openly negotiate with Israel.

His links with the PLO also blew hot and cold. He attempted to pressure Arafat to agree to UN Resolution 242, which called for Israel to withdraw from "occupied territories" and referred to the Palestinians as "refugees." Arafat rejected this, refusing to recognize Israel's right to exist, feeling that the territory from which Israel was to withdraw must be more clearly spelled out, and that the Palestinians must be recognized as a people with a nation. Meantime, Hussein also passionately argued that a peace agreement for the region must include the PLO or a spokesperson for the Palestinians.

Abdullah was aware of the ongoing tension. He had attended an Armored Officers Advanced Course at Fort Knox, Kentucky, in the United States in 1985, then returned to Jordan to assume command of a tank company in the 91st Armored Brigade of the Jordanian Armed Forces. He now had attained the rank of captain. The fearless Abdullah repeatedly demonstrated his skill and talent under difficult circumstances, also serving with the Royal Jordanian Airforce Anti-Tank Wing, where he received his wings and his qualifications as a Cobra Attack Pilot.

He briefly interrupted his military career to attend the School of Foreign Service at Georgetown University in Washington, D.C. Pursuing a Masters of Science in Foreign Service degree, Abdullah undertook advanced study and research in international affairs as a Mid-Career Fellow. He then returned to Jordan and his military career.

JORDAN GIVES UP THE WEST BANK

December 1987 marked the beginning of a violent Palestinian uprising against Israeli forces in the West Bank and Gaza, known as the *intifada* (or "shaking off"). Hussein was devastated when his efforts to promote Palestinian involvement in the Middle East peace process were responded to by threats from Palestinian leaders who urged their people to reject any links with Jordan.

Since 1917, the Hashemite family had claimed Palestine as their right, as an integral part of their kingdom. On December 31, 1988, however, King Hussein severed all political and administrative ties between Jordan and the West Bank, bringing that claim to an end. The House of Representatives (half of whose members were Palestinian) was dissolved. Jordanian public service employees in the West Bank (such as teachers and government officials) were dismissed.

"Let them have it," Hussein reportedly told the commander in chief of the Jordanian army. "Let them carry the burden." Hussein reserved claim only to the holy places in Jerusalem, to which he felt a spiritual and personal, as well as political, commitment.

On November 15, the PLO proclaimed an independent State of Palestine and announced its endorsement of UN Resolution 252. Jordan was one of 61 nations to recognize the new state.

The pullout had immediate economic consequences for Jordan. The value of its currency, the *dinar*, dropped severely. The king was forced to agree to price increases on nearly all basic goods and services. Unemployment skyrocketed. Antigovernment riots followed. The climate of dissatisfaction was so high that the prime minister and cabinet all resigned, and the king was forced to call for a full general election for the first time since 1967 (although political parties were still banned). The election was held on November 8, 1989, and resulted in a clear victory for Islamists and other "opposition" representatives.

WAR IN THE GULF

On August 2, 1990, the leader of Iraq, Saddam Hussein, suddenly invaded Kuwait. King Hussein had been an ally of

An American Education

Saddam Hussein's, but he was caught in the middle when the leader invaded Kuwait, and attempted to mediate without issuing a firm condemnation of the invasion.

The U.S. embargo of Iraq had implications for Jordan's economy: Many Jordanians worked in Iraq and Kuwait. Jordan had benefited from free Iraqi oil in exchange for loans during Iraq's eight-year war with Iran. Jordan's route to Iraq was closed to trade. Hussein attempted to invoke the Arab League as the only practical mediator in the conflict, but Saudi Arabia, Egypt, and Syria refused, arguing that international action was the only way to halt Iraq. Hussein's efforts at peacemaking failed, and on January 16, 1991, an international coalition launched an attack on Iraq to force its withdrawal from Kuwait—an attack that King Hussein condemned.

Little more than a decade later, Hussein's son, Abdullah, would find himself forced to carefully choose his diplomatic position in face of a U.S.-led coalition attacking Iraq. King Hussein's position drew international criticism for his unwillingness to openly condemn Saddam Hussein. In his case, the Gulf War conflict divided Arab nations. His son would find his diplomatic footing easier, as Arab nations and much of the world joined in opposing the attack against Iraq.

After the war ended, Jordan continued to maintain ties with Iraq, although King Hussein and Saddam Hussein would not have called each other allies. Jordanians returned to Iraq to work; Iraq restored much of its supply of oil to Jordan (a relationship exempt from the oil sanctions imposed by coalition forces).

THE PEACEMAKING PROCESS

With the end of the first Gulf War, achieving a peaceful resolution to the Middle East conflict became an international priority. King Hussein participated in a peace summit in Madrid in 1991 with Israel and its neighbors, one in which the negotiations focused on linking Jordanians and Palestinians as a single negotiating team. But in the months that followed, Jordan was shut out as Palestinians and Israelis continued negotiating secretly.

Hussein was outraged when he learned of the secret negotiations between Israel and the PLO. Whereas once Jordan and the Palestinians had been necessary to negotiate peace with Israel, now it appeared that the PLO was negotiating its own, separate arrangement with Israel.

Hussein soon recognized, however, that Jordan was no longer under any obligation to coordinate with the PLO or to link peacemaking efforts to the Palestinian cause. Jordan could cut its own deal with the Israelis and take the lead in the peacemaking process. This became a greater priority for King Hussein as health problems began to mark his reign. In the fall of 1992 he traveled to the Mayo Clinic in Minnesota, for tests—tests that later revealed the presence of precancerous cells in his ureter. Doctors removed the cells, and the prognosis seemed good. After five weeks away from Jordan, spent recovering and meeting with President George H.W. Bush in Washington and Queen Elizabeth in England, the king and his wife returned to Jordan.

It was apparently following this brush with his mortality that King Hussein first contemplated his succession, reconsidering the plan he had made decades earlier to provide for an orderly transition in leadership following his death. Although Hussein's brother, Hassan, remained crown prince, Hussein began to consider the question of who among his family might be best able to rule Jordan when he was gone.

King Hussein favored the idea of the creation of a "family council," a gathering of select family members who would meet and decide together who might be the best ruler after King Hussein's death. This type of decisionmaking by consensus was not uncommon in the Arab world, or in Islam, and Hussein apparently believed that this approach might ensure family unity and help ensure that the family, "not only stand together and work together, but that the most suitable person *willing* to assume the responsibility is chosen." The move to a family council would require Hussein to amend Jordan's Constitution, which since 1965 had specified that the king would be succeeded by his oldest son or a brother.

Hussein's illness had also given him a new sense of urgency about bringing a peaceful end to the conflict with Israel. On July 25, 1994, King Hussein and Israel's prime minister, Yitzhak Rabin, formally announced the ending of the hostilities that had existed between their countries since 1948 in a meeting in Washington, D.C. King Hussein's brother, Crown Prince Hassan, had been instrumental in the early stages of the negotiations. American president Bill Clinton helped close the deal by offering the forgiveness of Jordanian debt of hundreds of millions of dollars and military aid designed to modernize the Jordanian military.

The agreement was finally concluded when Yitzhak Rabin made a surprise visit to Amman in early October 1994, and the final peace treaty was signed on October 26, on the border between Israel and Jordan in Wadi Araba. The treaty acknowledged King Hussein as the custodian of the Holy Places in Jerusalem, and contained a clause by which Israel returned 116 square miles of desert to Jordan. In a critical clause, Israel agreed to recognize Jordan's "sovereignty, territorial integrity, and political independence" and to "refrain from the use of force or weapons, conventional, non-conventional or of any other kind." Hussein viewed this as his most important accomplishment as king, providing Jordan with a safety it had not known for four decades.

Both Hussein and Rabin delivered emotional speeches when the treaty was signed. King Hussein declared, "This is a day like no other in terms of hopes, in terms of promise, and in terms of determination. It is the dawning of the era of peace, mutual respect between us all, tolerance, and the coming together of people here and for generations to come to build and achieve what is worthy of them." Rabin's comments on the October 26 signing included these stirring words:

> As dawn broke this morning and a new day began, new life came into the world. Babies were born in Jerusalem. Babies were born in Amman. But this morning is different. To the mother of the Jordanian newborn, a blessed day to you. To the mother of the Israeli newborn, a blessed day to you. The peace that was born today gives us the hope that children born today will never know war between us, and their mothers will know no sorrow.

A year later, Yitzhak Rabin was dead, assassinated by an Israeli. King Hussein and Queen Noor flew to Jerusalem for Rabin's funeral. It was Hussein's first visit to the city since the 1967 war. Hussein's tribute was emotional:

> I had never thought that the moment would come like this when I would grieve the loss of a brother, a colleague, and a friend—a man—a soldier—who met us on the opposite side of a divide. You lived as a soldier, you died as a soldier for peace. I commit before you, before my people in Jordan, before the world, myself to continue to do our utmost to ensure that we leave a similar legacy. And when my time comes, I hope it will be like my grandfather's, and like Yitzhak Rabin's.

A COURAGEOUS WARRIOR

As his father gained prominence in the world as a man of peace, Abdullah was gaining prominence in Jordan as a military officer. By 1994, he was promoted to the rank of brigadier and was appointed commander of Jordan's elite Special Forces.

During a 1995 trip to the United States as part of a military delegation, Abdullah was invited by a friend to visit the

Paramount Studios set of "Star Trek: Voyager" in Los Angeles. Abdullah was a fan of the show, and looked forward to the visit. To his surprise, when he visited the set, he was invited to put on a uniform and make-up and become an extra, playing one of the crewmembers. Abdullah was pleased that as a crewmember his military rank was promoted to that of commodore.

In 1996, the Special Forces incorporated the Royal Guard, military intelligence, and special operations, all into a single, highly skilled unit. The brigade's brief was expanded to include internal security assignments, counterterrorism missions, unconventional warfare missions, and conventional and non-conventional military operations deemed beyond the scope of Jordan's army. The unit also trained other army units in special operations.

In 1998, Abdullah gained public attention when he led commandos in storming the hideout of gunmen who had killed eight people, including the charge d'affaires of the Iraqi Embassy in Jordan. Honoring his courage in the raid, King Hussein promoted him to major general.

Abdullah occasionally served as his father's deputy, traveling to Washington to assist in negotiations for military assistance. For the most part, however, their careers seemed separate, with Abdullah focusing on Jordan's military while his father focused on a more peaceful future.

THE TIME HAS COME

Hussein's efforts for peace became, in a sense, his lasting legacy. In July of 1998, he returned to the Mayo Clinic, having been diagnosed with lymphatic cancer. For six months he remained in the United States for treatment, while his brother, Crown Prince Hassan, ruled as regent in his absence. While he was undergoing treatment, he was persuaded by President Bill Clinton to travel to the Wye River in Maryland to lend his presence to tension-filled negotiations between Israeli leader Benjamin Netanyahu and Yasser Arafat. The negotiations had

Palestinian leader Yasser Arafat, President Bill Clinton, and Israeli Prime Minister Benjamin Netanyahu applaud King Hussein in the White House, Washington, D.C., on October 23, 1998, where the West Bank accord was to be signed. After a long night of talks between Israelis and Palestinians, Netanyahu and Arafat agreed on a breakthrough land-for-peace deal on the West Bank, the culmination of nine days of intense negotiations mediated by President Clinton. King Hussein worked tirelessly for years to bring the parties together.

stalled, and Clinton hoped that Hussein's presence might spark renewed energy for the meeting.

Hussein arrived at the Wye River meeting on October 19. Most of those present had not realized the extent of his illness, and the sight of the thin, bald, weak king was a shocking revelation to those on both sides. "You cannot afford to fail," Hussein told Arafat and Netanyahu and their aids. "You owe this to your people, to your children, to future generations." Hussein's presence helped spark the negotiating process at the meeting, and the Wye River Accords concluded with a promise of Israeli withdrawal from more West Bank land in return for security safeguards from the Palestinians. The accords were suspended two months later by Israel, however, and the Netanyahu government failed shortly after.

In January 1999, Hussein returned to Jordan, claiming that his health had improved—a claim that quickly proved false. Upon his return, King Hussein determined to change his plans for succession. After serving 34 years as crown prince, Hussein's brother, Hassan, was no longer next in line for the throne. Instead, Hussein chose his oldest son, Abdullah.

It is not clear precisely why Hussein chose to name Abdullah as his successor, although there are several likely scenarios. His dissatisfaction with Hassan's decisionmaking while he was undergoing treatment at the Mayo Clinic was mentioned earlier, and he was suspicious that Hassan had been behind the smear campaign against Queen Noor that had transpired during Hussein's absence from the country. Prince Hamzah was believed by many to be his favorite son, but experts suggest that, having himself known the difficulty of becoming king as a teenager, Hussein did not wish to place that same burden on the young Hamzah.

In contrast, naming his oldest son crown prince would not require an amendment to the Constitution. Abdullah had earned the respect of many Jordanians for his exceptional military service. He had experience with command, and a firm knowledge of the West from his years of schooling. He had formed friendships with many who would become the next generation of leaders in the Middle East. At 36, he was mature and polished. He was a logical choice. And while he was still alive, Hussein could make provisions for Hamzah's eventual succession by insisting that Abdullah appoint Hamzah as crown prince when Abdullah ascended to the throne.

Hours after his announcement, Hussein's health began once more to fail, and he flew back to the Mayo Clinic. Medical

King Abdullah's wife, Princess Rania (left), with Queen Noor, in front of the late King Hussein's grave at the royal cemetery in Amman, March 1999, just a month after Hussein's death from cancer. King Abdullah later gave his wife the title of Queen, allowing Noor to retain the same title, but with fewer privileges.

treatment was not successful, though, and Queen Noor was determined that her husband's final hours would be spent in his own country. Hussein died in Amman on February 7, 1999. His son, Abdullah, was now the king of a country whose people had, for the most part, known only one king: his father. After 46 years, the challenge was now for Abdullah to preserve the Hashemite rule while shaping the monarchy in his own image.

CHAPTER

6

The New King

King Abdullah II was 37 years old when he became the ruler of the Hashemite Kingdom of Jordan. Most Jordanians knew him as a military hero. They knew that he, like his father, had a daredevil reputation—relaxing as a qualified reconnaissance diver, pilot, and free-fall parachutist or by racing automobiles (Abdullah holds a Jordanian National Rally Racing Championship). They knew that he enjoyed water sports and scuba diving. But these were sketchy details, little match for the decades most Jordanians had spent with Hussein as their king.

The first challenge he faced was in moving past the legacy left by his father. In the 46 years of his reign, King Hussein had become inextricably linked with the land he ruled; he was in many ways the public face that represented Jordan to the world. Now Abdullah II had to present a different face to his people and the world, and begin to shape a new legacy for Jordan as it entered the twenty-first century.

According to Robert Satloff, executive director of the Washington Institute for Near East Policy, Hussein was one of the remarkable leaders of the second half of the twentieth century, known for being a survivor, for infusing humanity and substance into the making of peace, and for making of Jordan a "real country," a country that could survive without him.

The new king, bearing the name of his great-grandfather, the Hashemite who had first shaped Jordan into a monarchy, offered his people a new vision of royalty, and yet he was in many ways a composite of Jordan's past and future. With a British mother, he, like his country, had British heritage. He served in the military, and Jordan's armed forces played a critical role in the country's history and in its relation to neighboring countries in the Middle East.

Further, very significantly in a country whose population is more than half Palestinian, Abdullah had a Palestinian wife. He had married Rania Yassin, a middle-class Palestinian from a prominent West Bank family who had grown up in Kuwait and then been forced to relocate to Jordan following the Iraqi invasion in 1990. The wedding took place June 10, 1993. Now she was Queen Rania. At the time of his coronation, he had a son, Prince Hussein, born June 28, 1994, and a daughter, Princess Iman, born September 27, 1996. A second daughter, Princess Salma, would be born on September 26, 2000.

King Abdullah officially ascended to the throne February 7, 1999. He initially committed to carrying out the policies of his father—not an easy task. But Abdullah had inherited much of his father's charisma. He had many friends among the young royals of other Arab nations. He was athletic and daring, and he had developed close relations with Americans, thanks in part to his education in the United States.

Abdullah quickly took steps to pull the spotlight firmly on himself and his wife, making sure that neither Prince Hassan

King Abdullah II, with his family (from left to right): Prince Hussein, Princess Iman, Queen Rania, and Princess Salma, strolling on the beach in front of their summer palace in Aqaba in April 2001, as part of a documentary created for the Travel Channel.

nor his father's widow, Queen Noor, continued to serve as "official" spokespersons for the royal family, effectively sidelining them both. Both King Abdullah and Queen Rania were energetic and enthusiastic, making public appearances (with Abdullah speaking in his halting Arabic) and quickly adopting several important policy positions to distinguish the new, young, and glamorous royal couple from previous rulers.

Domestically, Abdullah quickly faced several challenges. The economy was still in a downturn, a state it had been in since the late 1980s and from which it had not completely recovered. Unemployment was high. The value of the dinar was weak, following uncertainty about the change in succession and the death of Hussein. Abdullah needed to take steps to restructure the economy—to proceed with steady liberalization in certain areas while providing social security for the 30 percent of Jordan's population living below the poverty line.

Externally, Abdullah faced challenges as well. Neighboring Iraq was headed by the belligerent Saddam Hussein, who periodically issued threats against any nations negotiating with Israel or the United States.

The country Abdullah inherited was far more politicized than the Jordan his father had first ruled. The military provided a strong, central security force—one that Abdullah needed to cultivate. Abdullah also needed to be mindful of the evolving role of tribes in Jordanian society, and how their changing role would impact economic and political developments in his kingdom.

A VIEW TO THE WORLD

Abdullah's initial focus was on foreign policy, working hard to cement Jordan's relations with many different nations and traveling to visit heads of state in the Gulf and in the United States. In previous generations, relations with Syria had been strained. Abdullah determined to change this by building a good relationship with Bashar al-Assad, next in line for the presidency of Syria (Bashar al-Assad became president of Syria in June 2000). Abdullah took advantage of the beginning of his reign to make a "meet and greet" tour of many different nations, using these visits as opportunities to strengthen or build new relationships with a number of countries.

The New King

Pope John Paul II is greeted by King Abdullah II at the Amman airport at the beginning of his weeklong pilgrimage through the Holy Land, in March 2000. The pope retraced the footsteps of Moses and Jesus and became only the second pope in history to visit Jerusalem.

One nation King Abdullah did wait to visit was Israel. It was 14 months after his accession that Abdullah finally traveled west to Israel for a public visit. The delay was not to mark a lessened commitment to the security agreements both nations had signed, but again to demonstrate that a new man was now ruling Jordan. His father had become closely linked with achieving peace with Israel; Abdullah wanted to begin to build his own legacy, separate and apart from his father.

In July 1999, a more leftist candidate, Ehud Barak, was elected prime minister of Israel. New accords were signed between Israel and the Palestinians, followed by more peace talks and a meeting between Barak and the Syrian foreign minister.

In August 1999, Abdullah expelled three leaders of the militant group Hamas from Jordan. Although the move won the approval of leadership in the United States, Israel, and the Palestinian Authority (the provisional government established in Palestinian territory), it sparked outrage among Palestinians living in Jordan, for whom Hamas's terrorist actions against Israel were viewed as heroic resistance. It was Abdullah's introduction to the tricky path the Jordanian ruler must negotiate between international diplomacy and domestic policymaking. However, Abdullah proved adept at handling the Palestinian leadership, avoiding the kind of sweeping claims to Jerusalem and the holy lands that had marked the rule of other Hashemites.

In 2000, Ehud Barak met with the Syrian foreign minister in Washington in an effort to cement peace between Israel and Syria. Peace between Israel and the Palestinian Authority also seemed possible in 2000, but Yasser Arafat proved inflexible, and the talks dissolved in disappointment. Soon afterward, Barak's government collapsed and the Syrian presidency changed hands. Then, in September 2000, the right-wing general Ariel Sharon made a volatile appearance at Jerusalem's Haram al-Sharif, the third-holiest site in Islam. The appearance sparked a second uprising or *intifada* among Palestinians. Several weeks later, Sharon was elected prime minister of Israel. Abdullah determined to postpone sending an ambassador to Tel Aviv until the furor over Sharon's election had quieted down. He intended to ensure that Jordan remained a critical player in the Middle East peace process.

THE CARING ROYALS

King Abdullah was determined to learn the true mood of his people—the way in which they really lived and their feelings

Prince Ghazi Ibn Muhammed, Prince Hamzah, and King Abdullah II listen to inhabitants of the village of Turki. King Abdullah likes to hear the thoughts of his subjects on the country and its leaders. He has even been known to secretly slip into the streets of Amman at night to talk to locals on a wide range of topics.

about their country and its leaders. He began to make unannounced visits to inspect state-run hospitals, and then, in disguise, would secretly slip into the streets of Amman at night to talk with Jordanians and find out their thoughts on a wide range of topics.

In a February 2003 interview with the British Broadcasting Corporation (BBC), Abdullah explained his reasons for these incognito trips:

> A lot of people that can be around leaders would like to tell them what they think they would like to hear. So you have a mental effort to break out of that—to keep going back to

reinforce what you think are the problems. So by travelling around it's just a reinforcement that this is a particular sector of society that needs help and since nobody knows who you are you can actually get a feeling whether the government is treating a citizen properly, whether the hospital is providing the right type of services and then I can go back and bring in individuals who are responsible and say "Look, you have been letting society down—letting Jordanians down, don't do it again."

Queen Rania quickly adopted a platform of speaking out against domestic violence and "honor killing"—the practice by which male family members murder female relatives found to have committed adultery or lost their virginity before marriage. Although not traveling in disguise like her husband, the queen also enjoyed speaking with her people in relaxed, informal settings. She often traveled to remote villages, unannounced, driving off in her car, followed by two security guards.

The couple founded the Jordanian Hashemite Charity Organization, an entity whose aim was to provide humanitarian aid to Palestinians living under Israeli occupation. Abdullah also founded the Socio-Economic Transformation Plan, which channeled funds from foreign aid and privatization of industries into education, health care, and job creation.

In addition to fostering their image as "the caring royals," Abdullah and Rania—particularly Rania—soon became known as the "glamorous royals." The queen was young—only 29 years old when her husband became king—and attractive. Her fashion sense and astute choice of designer clothing soon placed her on the front covers of fashion magazines. Like her husband, she was athletic, enjoying water skiing, running, and cycling.

She was also an intelligent and articulate spokesperson for the monarchy. Rania had been born in Kuwait on August 31, 1970, attending primary and secondary school in Kuwait before earning a degree in business administration from the American University in Cairo. She worked briefly in marketing at Citibank, then took a job in Amman, working for Apple Computer. She had met her future husband at a dinner party in January 1993. Two months later they were engaged, and within six months of their first meeting they were married.

Both Queen Rania and King Abdullah, for all their glamour, attempted to convey an image of a more populist approach to the monarchy. Toward this aim, the couple decided not to live in the palace but instead maintained a comfortable home in the suburbs of Amman. Their home provided a relaxing sanctuary where the couple could escape palace formality, surrounded by family photos and glass cases containing one of Abdullah's passions: a collection of firearms and ancient ornamental weapons.

AN EARLY STRUGGLE

Abdullah's inexperience was most evident in his ability to deal with Jordan's politicians. His father, as a young ruler, had experienced the same struggle, attempting to place his stamp on a class of political elite unwilling to compromise.

Abdullah, as king, needed to shape a government that reflected his own ideas and needs. In March 1999, he placed a conservative government in office, reporting to a new prime minister, Abdul Rauf al-Rawabdeh, who was known as "the bulldozer." As his Chief of the Royal Court, Abdullah chose a liberal, Abdul Karim al-Kabariti. The two men, in positions that required close cooperation, instead were continually at odds, fighting over press freedoms, economic liberalization, and women's rights. Ultimately, Kabariti resigned, and Abdullah was forced to replace Rawabdeh when he took steps to launch a conservative agenda to Jordan's politics. Later, in November 2003, Abdullah would eliminate the position of Chief of the Royal Court altogether, centralizing responsibility for both functions in the office of prime minister.

In his second cabinet, Abdullah chose more liberal representatives—politicians whose views and values more closely reflected his own, including Ali Abu Al-Ragheb as prime minister. Ragheb had built strong relationships with Palestinians living in Jordan and with members of the national assembly, and benefited from a private sector background that made him receptive to Abdullah's liberal plans for Jordan's economy.

Many of the policies designed to lead Jordan in the direction of liberalization had to be put on hold, however, when the second Palestinian *intifada* broke out. Security became more of a concern, and once more a dividing line emerged within the Jordanian population. Jordan's Anti-Normalization Committee —an activist organization—began publishing a "blacklist" containing the names of Jordanians—particularly public figures, politicians, and writers—who had interacted with Israel. As the disorder spread and grew more violent, Abdullah's focus became to ensure that the chaos did not spread across the border. Public protest was outlawed, control was more firmly centralized in Amman at the expense of local authorities, and the media was censored.

ECONOMIC REFORM

Although security was of paramount concern, Abdullah also quickly took steps to address Jordan's economic crisis. His approach was to look externally, as well as internally. Under Abdullah's leadership, in 2001, Jordan became the second country in the Middle East (after Israel) to negotiate a free-trade agreement with the United States. A Qualifying Industrial Zone was established near Irbid for the joint manufacture or processing of goods by Jordan and Israel for distribution to the United States duty- and quota-free.

Hoping to attract investment to Jordan's Red Sea coast, Abdullah helped launch the low-tax Aqaba Special Economic Zone in 2001. He also continued plans to privatize several state businesses, including the Royal Jordanian airline and

King Abdullah II meets with Israeli Foreign Minister Shimon Peres in Aqaba Palace, April 29, 2001. Peres was on a trip to Jordan and Egypt to discuss an Arab plan to put an end to seven months of violence between Israelis and Palestinians. Abdullah has continued his father's plan to seek peace with Israel.

Jordan Telecom. Jordan joined the World Trade Organization in 2000.

Abdullah also encouraged trade and business links with other Arab nations. In 2001, the national electricity grids of Jordan, Syria, and Egypt were linked in an attempt to share the cost of electricity generation. Construction of a dam between Jordan and Syria on the Yarmouk was begun.

Although these small economic successes were popular initiatives, the economy remained stagnant. In addition, Abdullah would soon face new diplomatic challenges, both at home and abroad, as he attempted to build strong relationships both with the West and the Arab world at a time when divisions between those two spheres grew vast.

U.S. President Bill Clinton and King Abdullah II witness the signing of an historic U.S.–Jordan Trade Agreement by U.S. Trade Representative Charlene Barshefsky (right) and Jordan's Deputy Prime Minister for Economic Affairs Dr. Mohammad Halaika (seated, center left) at the White House, October 24, 2000. The agreement, the first between the United States and an Arab nation, aimed to eliminate duties and commercial barriers to bilateral trade.

On the one-year anniversary of his accession to the throne, Abdullah delivered a speech in Amman, pledging his loyalty to his people and to Jordan. He also encouraged his people to remain open and supportive for the changes he envisioned for their homeland:

> Our ambitions are substantial but their achieving demands working in one homogeneous team, having a clear vision, a

comprehensive future perspective realizing this age's offerings, its scientific and technological achievements and the preparedness to acknowledge the swift-changing pace of these offerings, constantly and promptly. In order to enable ourselves to realize the spirit of this age and its challenges, we need to substantially review our policy plans . . . [and] educational training programs, . . . [and] rehabilitate our human resources, . . . in order to deal with the challenges facing this country, the outcome of the revolution of software and communication technology with confidence and the capability to be in line and interact with it. . . . My confidence in the future is great because it stems from my confidence in the creative Jordanian individual, the abilities and talents he has acquired, the science and knowledge he has armed himself with, and his untiring will that shuns despair or fear of change.

SEPTEMBER 11, 2001

King Abdullah was in a plane, traveling over Nova Scotia, when he first learned that an aircraft had crashed into one of the World Trade Center towers in New York City. He was traveling to the United States, planning to visit friends in Los Angeles, and then to meet with President George Bush and attend a meeting of the United Nations Security Council later in the week.

Eventually, Queen Rania managed to get a call through to Abdullah to inform him that what was thought to be an accident was actually a terrorist attack, involving four planes and targets in New York and Washington. Abdullah went immediately to the cockpit where the pilot turned on the BBC World Service and they learned the full extent of what was transpiring in the air. The plane turned around and returned to London to refuel. It was only then that Abdullah found a television set and saw for the first time the images of the aircrafts and the devastation in two American cities.

Abdullah quickly wrote a letter to the president of the United States, expressing his support and sympathy:

Mr. President,

The people of Jordan join the people of the United States in our absolute condemnation of the terrorist aggression against your nation. Our hearts reach out to the victims and their families, and we honor the selfless men and women who have risked their lives to aid the injured and suffering.

Be assured that the Hashemite Kingdom of Jordan, its leaders and people stand with you against the perpetrators of these terrorist atrocities. We denounce the violence and hatred they represent.

Together, Jordan and the United States have worked for a better world. Together, we will work to ensure that the enemies of peace and freedom do not prevail.

The king's visit to the United States was postponed until September 27, when he became the first Arab leader to meet the American president since the September 11 attacks—attacks that were linked to the terrorist network al Qaeda, led by Osama bin Laden. Abdullah was quick to publicly proclaim his support for President Bush's "war on terrorism," but also urged the president not to allow the terrorists to make the war a conflict between the West and Islam. He linked the attacks to political violence in the Middle East, urging the president to address what he believed to be the root cause of violence in the region and anti-Western sentiment in the Muslim world: the Palestinian issue.

It is not surprising that Abdullah believed that the Palestinian crisis was the root cause of conflict in the Middle East. As Jordan entered the twenty-first century, its king continued to try to build bridges with the West and with neighboring countries, all in an effort to attempt to create a stable region as a framework for growth in Jordan. He also began to assume a role once held by his father—that of becoming the visible and moderate voice representing the Palestinian cause. As early as April 9, 2001, in an interview with Jim Lehrer on the PBS television program "NewsHour," Abdullah noted presciently:

> You have to understand that the images we see on television every day of the violence in the territories has created tremendous frustration, not only at the leadership level, but more importantly at the street level in the Middle East. . . .
>
> His late Majesty used to say, we want peace for our children and their children. I'd like to modify that to say, I want peace for us now and our children. This is a new millennium. Let's start it right. The idea of Israel being integrated into the region, for us to be able to break down the barriers and live in peace and prosperity once and for all—that's why it's so important for us, and why it's so important for the United States.

CHAPTER

7

A Vision of Change

With the beginning of the twenty-first century, King Abdullah presided over a country whose security had become a greater priority than it ever had been before. Anti-American and anti-Western violence was on the rise in Jordan; Abdullah responded with even greater controls over the press and speech and by ensuring that the punishment for terrorist crimes was severe.

Abdullah also focused on economic improvement, while building the image of Jordan at home and abroad. He made an effort to build consensus within the many different factions of the kingdom, to encourage his people to view themselves as Jordanians first, rather than to allow ethnic, religious or tribal identity to become paramount.

In an April 2001 interview on the PBS show "NewsHour," King Abdullah noted what he believed was the greatest challenge he had faced in his first two years as king:

I think changing the mentalities of people that, no matter how difficult the future looks, whatever obstacles we have in front of us, they can be overcome. There's always the attitude it can't be done, it's too difficult. That doesn't sit very well with me. And now there's a sense of teamwork in Jordan; there's a sense that we can achieve the prosperity that we want, and that's being permeated—all sectors of society. We're moving forward, and I think the biggest challenge at the beginning was to get people to believe that the vision I have for Jordan is possible and can be reached.

Abdullah frequently noted that he had once been responsible for four people (his immediate family) and then had become responsible for four million people. His growing skill at the management of his country and his comfort in the role of king was evident as he gained confidence in policymaking.

The economy received particular attention, and Abdullah made an effort to ensure that Jordan was receptive to emerging businesses and technologies and supportive of a younger generation of entrepreneurs. In an interview with the BBC in 2003, Abdullah noted his efforts to encourage the development of information technology (IT) specialists in Jordan:

What we are trying to do is create opportunities in Jordan with investment, reaching out to international companies to create a centre of excellence in Jordan so that the Jordanian has the opportunity to stay in his country. In the IT market, the IT companies have doubled in the past 18 months. Two or three major companies that were run by Jordanians have come back from the Gulf and even the United States because we are setting the foundations to give them advantages to stay in Jordan. . . . [W]e are looking at a very strong courageous economic reform program for 2002. It's aimed at not only creating more jobs but opportunities in the high-tech sector to keep the talent back in Jordan. This is something that we have been trying to do from day one. The market has improved. We have identified IT technologies as a growth market—it has doubled in the size of companies and personnel in 18 months.

Abdullah also skillfully built strong ties with the United States, receiving in return substantial amounts of American dollars and aid. In 2003, Jordan followed only Israel, Egypt, and Colombia on the list of top recipients of U.S. aid. Following the September 11, 2001, attack, Jordan provided the United States with intelligence on the terrorist group responsible for the attack, al Qaeda. In addition, Jordanian troops—particularly mine-clearance and medical teams—formed part of the international coalition working in Afghanistan after al Qaeda and the Taliban regime that hosted them were routed in a U.S.-led attack. The strong ties would be tested, however, by a war that sparked outrage in the Arab world—the 2003 U.S.-led invasion of Iraq to oust its leader, Saddam Hussein.

THE WAR NEXT DOOR

On March 19, 2003, American forces (supported by a coalition of representatives from 35 nations) launched an attack on Iraq, designed to topple the regime of Saddam Hussein. American president George W. Bush outlined the reasons for the war in his public address when the military action began:

> My fellow citizens, at this hour American and coalition forces are in the early stages of military operations to disarm Iraq, to free its people, and to defend the world from grave danger. On my orders, coalition forces have begun striking selected targets of military importance to undermine Saddam Hussein's ability to wage war. These are opening stages of what will be a broad and concerted campaign. . . . The people of the United States and our friends and allies will not live at the mercy of an outlaw regime that threatens the peace with weapons of mass murder.

A Vision of Change   101

King Abdullah II greets Iraqi Vice President Taha Yassin Ramadan in Amman, September 2002. Ramadan was on a diplomatic offensive against Washington's threat to oust Iraqi leader Saddam Hussein. Jordan, the fourth-largest recipient of U.S. aid worldwide, remained neutral in the U.S.-led war in Iraq.

King Abdullah had met with Iraqi representatives of Saddam Hussein in the days and weeks before the war began; they asked him for his advice in resolving the pending conflict. These meetings left him with a clear sense that the Iraqi leadership lacked the vision to deal with the international community in a way that would avoid the crisis. In an interview with CNN after the war broke out, King Abdullah noted that he had explicitly explained to the Iraqi representatives that their only option was to cooperate and abide by UN resolutions.

"In each case the government official who came to see me said, 'Well, I can't tell Saddam that,'" Abdullah noted. "And I said, 'Then why are you here in the first place? If you're not going to get the message back to the leadership, you're wasting your time and you're wasting ours.'"

The attack was not universally supported. Neighboring nations were concerned not only by the conflict but by what it might unleash—those who might rise to power in Iraq once Saddam Hussein's dictatorship had ended and the creation of a new wave of anti-American and anti-Western violence. The initial round of military action quickly subdued Hussein's armies, and Hussein himself was captured, but conflict continued in Iraq as the coalition forces struggled to maintain order and install a new Iraqi government.

King Abdullah expressed his concern at the ongoing occupation of neighboring Iraq, and by the conflict that continued to mark a lack of control in many parts of the country. In the May 24, 2004, issue of *Newsweek*, he noted his concern about the ripples the war had created:

> What worries me is that there is tremendous anti-American sentiment throughout the Middle East and the world. It's the image people see of Israeli tanks with Palestinians and American tanks with Iraqis. It's these images that make people suspicious and frustrated toward what they perceive as a one-sided American policy.
>
> We are working hard for a unified Arab position against extremism and terrorism targeting innocent civilians, which means suicide bombers. We went to the Arab countries and said, 'Look, you need to come together with a blueprint for Arab reform. If you do not articulate such a blueprint, one may be forced upon you.' We in Jordan are in the clear: we have our plans and are not using regional problems as an excuse. We are moving forward, as are some of the other moderate countries. But the rest of you, wake up! The Middle East is changing.

A Vision of Change

U.S. President George W. Bush (second from right) walks with (left to right) Palestinian Prime Minister Mahmoud Abbas, Israeli Prime Minister Ariel Sharon, and King Abdullah II of Jordan at the conclusion of the Red Sea Summit, a Middle East peace initiative hosted by King Abdullah in June 2003.

King Abdullah also noted his concern about what would happen in the region should the United States fail to create a stable government in Iraq:

> The worst-case scenario of losing in Iraq is civil war there, which will draw everybody into the fray. Extremists will use an unstable Iraq. We have seen in history what Lebanon was like during its civil war, but this would be 10 times worse. [U.S. officials] must get the transition right. If they don't, we are in for serious trouble.

King Abdullah expressed his concern over the chaos in Iraq, but he refused to bow to pressure to send in Jordanian troops. Hosting the World Economic Forum in Jordan, the king noted that neighboring countries should not send in peacekeeping troops to Iraq to avoid the temptation to use them to "improperly influence Iraqi society."

"I've taken the decision, truly, from a moral point of view, that I don't think it's right for Jordan to send troops to Iraq," the king said. "And I don't think it's right, at the same time, for anybody else (bordering Iraq).... We have our special interests. It is right for Arab troops to be committed, but not those that surround Iraq—it's better for us to sit this one out."

THE CHALLENGES OF GEOGRAPHY

Iraq is merely one example of the challenges posed by Jordan's location. Jordan has traditionally been the weaker nation surrounded by stronger neighbors, and when conflict or chaos breaks out in one of those neighboring countries, there is a very real threat of the trouble seeping across the border.

With Iraq to its east, Israel to its west, Syria to its north, and Saudi Arabia to its south, the kings of Jordan have learned to develop a balanced stance for their nation, and Abdullah has proved no exception. With a country whose population is half-Palestinian, Abdullah has continued to direct world attention to the Palestinian situation as a kind of blueprint to resolve conflict throughout the Middle East.

In a 2001 interview with the BBC, King Abdullah noted, "Jordan enjoys relations with everybody and this is, I think, the secret of Jordan—being able to have the confidence of both sides. And so from the start of the difficulties [in Palestinian territory]—even before the intifada with the peace process—Jordan was playing an active role of trying to bridge the difficulties or the differences between both sides."

The crisis in the West Bank is an ongoing challenge for King Abdullah. When conflict breaks out, more Palestinians flee into the kingdom, creating even greater strains on the economy and on existing resources and social services. The king has consistently noted his opposition to the idea of Jordan as a "host" for Palestinian refugees:

> We do not accept an exodus of Palestinians out of the West Bank into Jordan. Firstly, it is detrimental to the Palestinian cause. If there are no Palestinians in the West Bank, how can they secure a future homeland for themselves? And again the limitations of Jordan—it is not just the economy—it comes simply down to the amount of water that Jordan can provide to its citizens and so any increase of numbers or exodus from the West Bank into Jordan is a red line for our country. Obviously we have the responsibility to try and help those in the region, but Jordan is moving forward no matter what is happening.

A LOOK AHEAD

The challenges facing King Abdullah are great. Jordan is in a dangerous neighborhood, and the king must continue the diplomatic tradition so skillfully demonstrated by his father in ensuring that his country maintains strong ties with the West while building alliances with other Arab nations. Ongoing unrest in the West Bank and in Iraq has caused tourism revenues to plummet and has made security a top priority. The large number of Palestinian refugees continues to strain Jordan's resources. Economic prosperity still seems far away.

And yet the king has always projected a positive, hopeful image, both at home and abroad. He has noted the value of his position, at the forefront of a new generation of younger Arab leaders who are unburdened by "the same baggage as our fathers . . . that allows us to move beyond what trapped the older generations."

King Abdullah addresses the participants of the World Economic Forum in South Shoneh on the Dead Sea during the closing plenary, May 2004. This Middle East meeting sought to engage business and government in a process focused on implementing policy reform.

At the World Economic Forum, held in Jordan in May 2004, King Abdullah delivered the opening remarks, which reflected the legacy he hoped to leave in Jordan:

> I believe that the Arab world is in a unique position to forge a new, consensus-driven vision—a vision of change. . . . The approach I suggest looks forward, not to a remote and distant future, but to an attainable new present. And it is a comprehensive approach; one that deals with the region's core needs: peace based on justice; progress based on reform.
>
> This vision is, in one sense, not new. It rests on Islam's age-old humanistic values. Our heritage teaches us that human potential prospers where there is freedom, tolerance and mutual respect. . . . true Islam supports a democratic environment that respects human life, human rights, and the rule of law. It upholds accountable, transparent governance. These are the values that make people shareholders in, and protectors of, society.
>
> As we move forward with a regional consensus on reform, we must keep our eyes on the prize: real and effective improvement in people's lives.

CHRONOLOGY

1962 Abdullah bin Al Hussein is born on January 30 in Amman and is named crown prince.

1965 Fearing violence, King Hussein changes the royal succession and names his brother, Hassan, crown prince, on April 1.

1967 Abdullah enrolls in St. Edmund's School in Surrey, Great Britain.

1972 King Hussein divorces Abdullah's mother, Princess Muna, and marries Princess Alia.

1980 Abdullah joins Royal Military Academy Sandhurst in the United Kingdom.

1981 Commissioned as second lieutenant.

1984 Joins Jordanian Armed Forces; serves as platoon commander and company second-in-command in 40th Armored Brigade.

1986 Attaining the rank of captain, becomes commander of a tank company in the 91st Armored Brigade. Also serves with the Royal Jordanian Airforce Anti-Tank Wing, receiving his wings and his qualifications as a Cobra attack pilot.

1987 Attends School of Foreign Service at Georgetown University.

1993 Marries Rania Al-Yasin on June 10.

1994 Promoted to brigadier; becomes commander of elite Special Forces; son Hussein born June 28.

1996 Daughter Iman born September 27.

1998 Following daring commando raid, is promoted to major general.

1999 Becomes crown prince. On the death of his father, becomes king February 7.

2000 Daughter Salma born on September 26.

2000 Jordan joins World Trade Organization.

2001 Following September 11 attacks on United States, Jordan provides Americans with intelligence on al Qaeda terrorist group.

2003 Abdullah meets with representatives sent by Saddam Hussein in a futile effort to prevent American-led coalition attack to oust Hussein's regime in Iraq.

2004 Abdullah meets with American president George Bush to advise on transition to self-government in Iraq and continues to press for resolution of Palestinian crisis.

FURTHER READING

Books

Bell, Gertrude. *The Desert and the Sown.* New York: Cooper Square Press, 2001.

Fromkin, David. *A Peace to End All Peace.* New York: Avon Books, 1989.

Jehl, Douglas. "King Hussein Selects Eldest Son, Abdullah, as Successor," *New York Times*, January 26, 1999.

Keay, John. *Sowing the Wind: The Seeds of Conflict in the Middle East.* New York: W.W. Norton & Company, 2003.

Noor, Queen. *Leap of Faith.* New York: Miramax Books, 2003.

Robins, Philip. *A History of Jordan.* New York: Cambridge University Press, 2004.

Teller, Matthew. *The Rough Guide to Jordan.* 2nd ed. London: Rough Guides Ltd., 2002.

Wallach, Janet. *Desert Queen.* New York: Anchor Books, 1996.

Weymouth, Lally. "Time to 'Wake Up!' " *Newsweek* (May 24, 2004): 36.

Websites

Embassy of the Hashemite Kingdom of Jordan, Washington, D.C.
Jordanembassyus.org

English Version of the *Jordan Times*
Jordantimes.com

Official Website for King Abdullah II
Kingabdullah.jo

Online Interview with King Abdullah II
Kinghussein.gov.jo/98_aug12.html

INDEX

Aaron, 22
Abdullah I, King (great-grandfather), 40–55
   and advisors, 44
   and Arab Legion, 53
   and Arab Revolt, 27, 28, 31
   assassination of, 18, 55, 56, 58
   and children, 56. *See also* Nayif, Prince; Talal, King
   and East Bank, 54–55
   and East Jerusalem, 54
   and Egypt, 51
   and Great Britain, 32–33, 35, 36, 37–38, 40–41, 43–50
   and independence of Transjordan, 50
   and Israeli invasion, 51–54
   as king, 50
   and marriages, 56
   and Mesopotamia (Iraq), 33, 35, 36, 51
   and official recognition as emir, 46
   and Palestine, 36, 37, 49–50, 51, 54
   and Palestinians, 53, 54–55, 61
   and Saudis, 36, 46, 51
   and self-government, 48–49
   and Sharif Hussein in Transjordan, 46–47
   and Soviet Union, 51
   and succession, 56–58
   and Syria, 36–37, 50–51
   and temporary governance of Transjordan, 18, 37–39, 43–46
   and tribal conflict, 40–41
   and United States, 51
   and West Bank, 54–55
   and World War II, 50
Abdullah II, King, 82, 83–107
   and becoming king, 21, 24, 56, 82, 83, 84
   birth of, 14, 16, 24, 63
   as brigadier, 78, 79
   and Bush, 95, 96
   as captain, 73
   as caring royal, 88–91
   children of, 56, 84
   as crown prince, 14, 19, 21, 63, 64, 81
   as daredevil, 83
   and East *versus* West Bank, 54
   and economy, 86, 92–95, 99–100, 105
   and education, 64–65, 69–70, 71, 73, 81, 84
   and electricity, 93
   family of, 16–18, 24. *See also* Hussein, King
   and firearms and ancient weapons collection, 91
   as first lieutenant, 71
   and future, 105, 107
   as glamorous royal, 90–91
   and government, 91–92
   and Hamzah as crown prince, 19, 81
   and home in Amman, 91
   and information technology, 99–100
   and Iraq, 75, 86, 100–104
   and Israel, 87–88
   in Jordanian military, 19, 73, 91
   as major general, 79
   and marriage, 19, 84–86, 90–91, 95
   and military, 86
   and military career, 69–70, 71–72, 73, 78–79, 81, 83
   and one-year anniversary of accession to throne, 94–95
   and Palestinians, 60, 84, 88, 90, 92, 96–97, 104–105
   and part of military delegation in United States, 78–79

INDEX

powers of, 14, 16
and providing Americans with intelligence on al Qaeda, 100
and raid on gunmen, 79
as second lieutenant, 70
and September 11, 2001 attacks, 95–96, 100
and Syria, 86
and terrorism, 95–96, 98, 100
and tribes, 86
and United States, 100–104
and vision of royalty, 84–86, 94–95, 98–99, 105, 107
and West Bank, 105
and World Trade Organization, 93
Abir, Princess (adopted sister), 16, 68
Afghanistan, and Abdullah II, 100
Agence France Presse, 14
Aisha, Princess (sister), 16, 63
al-Aqsa Mosque, and assassination of Abdullah I, 55
Ali, Prince (stepbrother), 16, 17, 68, 70–71
Alia, Princess (stepmother), 16, 67–68, 69, 70
Alia, Princess (stepsister), 16, 63
Allenby bridge, 52, 53
al Qaeda, and September 11, 2001, 95–96, 100
Anglo-TransJordanian Treaty, 50, 51, 61
Anti-Normalization Committee, 92
Aqaba, 50
Aqaba Special Economic Zone, 92
Arab League, and Gulf War, 75
Arab Legion, 50, 53
Arab Revolt, 25, 27–29, 30, 31, 32, 33
Arafat, Yasser, 66, 72, 73, 79–81, 88
Assad, Bashar al-, 86

Balfour, Arthur, 31
Balfour Declaration, 31–32
Barak, Ehud, 88
Bedouins, 26, 41, 46, 62, 71
Bell, Gertrude, 26, 35
Bethlehem, 63
bin Laden, Osama, 96
Black September, 67, 68
British Broadcasting Corporation (BBC), Abdullah II's interview with, 89–90
Bruton, C.D., 40–41
Bush, George H.W., 76
Bush, George W., 95, 96, 100

caliph (sultan), 25
Carter, Jimmy, 72
Chamber of Deputies, 54
Chief of the Royal Court, 91
Christianity, 22
Churchill, Winston, 35–36, 37, 41, 44–45
civil war, and Hussein, 66–67, 68
Clinton, Bill, 77, 79, 80
Cold War, 61
Constantinople, 25, 28
Constitution
  of 1946, 58
  of 1952, 58
  and succession, 14, 19, 77, 81

Dead Sea, 23
Deerfield Academy (Deerfield, Massachusetts), Abdullah II attending, 70
Dina, Queen (stepmother), 16, 63
dinar, 74, 86
domestic violence, and Rania, 90

Eaglebrook School (Deerfield, Massachusetts), Abdullah II attending, 65, 69–70

111

INDEX

East Bank, 54–55, 63, 68
East Jerusalem, 54
economy, and Abdullah II, 86, 92–95, 99–100, 105
Egypt
    and Abdullah I, 51
    and electricity, 93
    and Great Britain, 25, 27, 30, 32
    and Gulf War, 75
    and Israel, 51, 53, 65
    and Jordan, 62
    and monarchy overthrown, 59
    and Nasser, 61, 62
    and Suez Crisis, 61–62
elections, and Hussein, 72
electricity, and Abdullah II, 93
Eliat, 65
Elizabeth, Queen, 76

Faisal, King
    and Arab Revolt, 27, 31, 33
    and kingdom in Syria, 32–33, 34, 36
    and Mesopotamia, 36, 37
Faisal, Prince (brother), 16, 63
family council, and succession, 76–77
fellaheen, 41
40th Armored Brigade, Abdullah II in, 71
France
    and division of Ottoman Empire, 30–32
    and Lebanon, 34
    and postwar occupation, 32–34
    and Suez Crisis, 61–62
    and Syria, 30, 32, 34, 36–37, 44, 48

Galilee, 54
Gardiner, Antoinette. *See* Muna, Princess
Gaza, 65, 73–74
George, David Lloyd, 41
Georgetown University (Washington, D.C.), Abdullah II attending School of Foreign Service at, 73
Golan Heights, 65
Gomorrah, 22
Gouraud, Henri, 44
Great Britain
    and Abdullah I, 33, 35–36, 37–39, 40–41, 43–50
    Abdullah II attending school in, 64, 69, 70, 71
    and Abdullah II in British Army, 70
    and Arab invasion of Israel, 52, 53
    and Arab Revolt, 27, 28–29, 33
    and division of Ottoman Empire, 30–32
    and Egypt, 25–27, 30, 32
    and fall of Ottoman Empire, 27
    and Hashemite rule in Middle East, 34–39, 40–41, 43–50
    and Hussein, 62
    Hussein attending school in, 59
    and India, 32, 35
    and Mesopotamia (Iraq), 30, 34–37
    and Palestine, 31–32, 34, 35, 41, 42, 44, 46, 47, 48, 49–50, 51
    and Persia (Iran), 30
    and postwar occupation of Middle East, 32–39, 40–41, 43–50
    and Sharif Hussein, 47
    and Suez Crisis, 61–62
    Talal attending school in, 56
    and Transjordan creation, 18, 24, 37

112

INDEX

Greece
  ancient, 22
  and Ottoman Empire, 25
Gulf War, 75

Habib, Randa, 14
hajj, 28
Halaby, Lisa. *See* Noor, Queen
Hamas, and Abdullah II, 88
Hamid, Sharifa Dina bin Abdul.
  See Dina, Queen
Hamzah, Prince (stepbrother), 16,
  18, 19–20, 71, 81
Haram al-Sharif, and Sharon, 88
Hashemites, 28
  and Arab Revolt, 27, 28, 29, 30,
    31, 32, 33
  and Muhammad, 53
  and Palestine, 74
  and rule in Middle East, 34–39
  and Saudis, 36, 46, 47.
    See also Abdullah I, King;
      Abdullah II, King; Faisal,
      King; Hussein, King; Hussein,
      Sharif
Hashim, Prince (stepbrother), 16
Hassan, Prince (uncle)
  and Abdullah II as king, 84–85
  as crown prince, 13–14, 16, 17,
    19–21, 63, 64, 76, 77, 81
  as regent, 11, 13–14, 70, 76, 79
Haya, Princess (stepsister), 16, 68
Hijaz, as Sharif Hussein's kingdom,
  29, 29–30, 31, 33, 46, 47
Hogarth, David, 35
honor killing, and Rania, 90
hospitals, Abdullah II visiting, 89
House of Representatives, 74
Hussein, King (father), 56–68,
  69–82
  and Abdullah II's military career,
    79

and Abdullah I's assassination,
  18, 55, 56, 58
and anti-Western policy, 61–62
and Arab alliances, 61–62
and assassination threats, 14, 64
and becoming crown prince, 18
and becoming king, 18, 59
birth of, 56
children of, 16–18, 63, 68
and civil war, 66–67, 68
and Cold War, 61
as daredevil, 83, 84
death of, 21, 82, 86
and East Bank, 63, 68
and education, 59
and elections, 72, 74
family of, 56
and government, 72, 74, 91
and Hassan as regent, 70, 76, 79
and Iraq, 74–75
and Israel, 33, 65–66, 72–74,
  75–78, 79–81, 87
legacy of, 83–84
and marriages, 16, 18, 19, 20, 21,
  63, 67–68, 69, 70, 71, 78, 81, 82
and military coup, 62
and Nayif as regent, 57–58
and 1967 war with Israel, 65–66
and Palestine Liberation
  Organization, 63–64, 66, 68,
  70, 72, 73
and Palestinians, 59–61, 63–64,
  66, 68, 73–74, 75–76
powers of, 14, 16
and prime ministers, 61
and succession, 12, 13–14, 16,
  17–21, 56, 64, 70–71, 76–77,
  81, 86
and Suez Crisis, 61–62
and suffering from lymphatic
  cancer, 12, 13–14, 17, 18–19,
  21, 76, 77, 79, 80

113

INDEX

and Syria, 65, 66
and United States aid, 62–63
and West Bank, 63, 64, 65, 73–74
and women, 72
and youngest brother Hassan as crown prince, 13–14, 16, 17, 19–21
Hussein, Prince (son), 84
Hussein, Saddam, 74–75, 86
   United States-led invasion ousting, 75, 100–104
Hussein, Sharif, 55
   and Arab Revolt, 27, 29, 31
   kingdom of, 29–30, 31, 33, 46, 47
   and Mecca, 27, 28
   and Palestine, 32
   and sons. See Abdullah I, King; Faisal, King
   in Transjordan, 46–47

Ibn Saud, 28, 36, 46, 47
Iman, Princess (daughter), 84
Iman, Princess (stepsister), 16
India, and Great Britain, 27, 32, 35
information technology (IT), and Abdullah II, 99–100
intifada
   1987, 73–74
   2000, 88, 92
Iraq
   and Abdullah I, 50–51
   and Abdullah II, 75, 86, 100–104
   coup in, 62
   and Faisal, 36, 37
   and Gulf War, 74–75
   and Hussein, 74–75
   and Israel, 51
   and Jordan's location, 24
   United States-led invasion of, 75, 100–104.
   See also Mesopotamia
Islam, 22, 24, 25, 28, 53

Islamic Educational College (Amman, Jordan), Abdullah II attending, 64
Israel
   and Abdullah I, 51–54
   and Abdullah II, 87–88
   and Arab invasion after statehood, 51–54
   and creation of new state, 51
   and Galilee, 54
   and Hamas, 88
   and Hussein, 14, 33, 65–66, 72–74, 75–78, 79–81, 87
   and Jerusalem, 51, 53, 54, 63, 65, 74, 77, 78, 88
   and Jordan's location, 24
   and "Land for Peace," 72
   and Negev Desert, 54
   and 1967 war, 65–66
   and Palestinian Authority, 88
   and peace treaty after Arab invasion, 53–54
   and Suez Crisis, 61–62
   and Syria, 65, 72, 88
   and trade with United States, 92
   and Zionism, 31, 33, 37, 48, 49.
   See also Palestine; Palestinians

Jerusalem, 51, 53, 54, 63, 65, 74, 77, 78, 88
Jesus, 22
Jews, 22.
   See also Israel; Palestine
John the Baptist, 22
Jordan
   and history, 22, 26. See also Middle East; Ottoman Empire; Transjordan
   and location, 24, 104
   and physical features, 23–24, 26–27
   Transjordan changed to, 53.
   See also Palestine

INDEX

Jordan River, 25, 26, 37, 43, 52, 53, 54, 65
Jordan Telecom, 93
Jordan Valley, 26
Jordanian Armed Forces, Abdullah II in, 71, 73
Jordanian Hashemite Charity Organization, 90
Jordanian National Rally Racing Championship, Abdullah II holding, 83

Kabariti, Abdul Karim al-, 91
Keay, John, 43
Kentucky, and Abdullah II attending Armored Officers Advanced Course at Fort Knox, 73
Kirkbride, Alec, 52
Kitchener, Lord, 28–29
Kuwait, Iraq's invasion of, 75

"Land for Peace," 72
Lawrence, T.E. (Lawrence of Arabia), 31, 33, 36, 44–46
League of Nations, 43
Lebanon
   and France, 30, 32, 34
   and Israel, 51
   Palestine Liberation Organization in, 66–67, 72
Legislative Council, 48–49
Lehrer, Jim, 97, 98–99
Lot, 22
Lydda, 53
lymphatic cancer, Hussein suffering from, 12, 13–14, 17, 18–19, 21, 76, 77, 79, 80, 81–82

McMahon, Sir Henry, 29
major general, Abdullah II as, 19

Massachusetts, and Abdullah II attending school in Deerfield, 65, 69–70
Mayo Clinic (Minnesota), Hussein in, 12, 13–14, 18, 21, 76, 81–82
Mecca
   and Ibn Saud, 47
   and Sharif Hussein, 27, 28
Mesopotamia (Iraq)
   and Abdullah I, 33, 35, 36
   and Arab Revolt, 29
   and British pledges of independence, 29
   and Faisal, 36, 37
   and Great Britain, 30, 34–37.
   See also Iraq
Middle East
   and Hashemite rule, 34–39.
      See also Abdullah I, King; Abdullah II, King; Faisal, King; Hussein, King; Hussein, Sharif
   and postwar occupation, 32–39, 40–41, 43–50.
   See also Ottoman Empire
military
   and Abdullah II as king, 86
   Abdullah II's career in, 69–70, 71–72, 73, 78–79, 81, 83
Minnesota, and Hussein in Mayo Clinic in Rochester, 12, 13–14, 18, 21, 76, 79, 81–82
Moses, 22
Muhammad, 22, 24, 25, 28, 53
Muhammad, Prince (uncle), 17
Muna, Princess (mother), 16, 24, 63, 67

Nabateans, 26
Nasser, Gamal Abdel, 61, 62

115

INDEX

Nayif, Prince (cousin), 56, 59
   as regent, 57–58
Negev Desert, 54
Netanyahu, Benjamin, 79–81
"NewsHour," Abdullah II interviewed on, 97, 98–99
Newsweek, 102
Noor, Queen (stepmother), 16, 18, 19, 20, 21, 70, 71, 78, 81, 82

oil
   and Great Britain, 27
   and Iraq, 75
Organic Law, 48
Ottoman Empire
   and Arab Revolt, 27, 28, 29, 30, 31, 32
   and Arab revolution, 25, 27–29
   division of, 29–32
   and loss of power, 25–27
   rule of, 24–27.
   See also Middle East
Oxford University (England), Abdullah II attending, 71

Palestine
   and Abdullah I, 36, 37, 49, 51
   and Arab Revolt, 29
   division of, 41, 46, 49–50, 51. *See also* Israel
   and Faisal, 33–34
   and Great Britain, 29, 31–32, 34, 35, 41, 42, 44, 46, 47, 48, 49–50, 51
   independent state of, 74
   as international sphere of influence, 30, 31
   and Jerusalem, 51
   and Jewish settlement, 31–32, 37, 43
   and 1967 war, 65
   and Sharif Hussein, 47

Palestine Liberation Organization (PLO)
   and Hussein, 63–64, 66, 68, 70, 73
   and independent State of Palestine, 74
   and Israel, 76
   in Lebanon, 66–67, 72
   and United Nations, 74
Palestinian Authority, 88
Palestinians
   and Abdullah I, 53, 54–55, 61
   and Abdullah II, 60, 84, 88, 90, 92, 96–97, 104
   and conflict with Zionists in Palestine, 49, 51
   and Hussein, 59–61, 63–64, 66, 68, 73, 73–74, 75–76
   and *intifada,* 73–74, 88, 92
   and Israel, 88
   in Lebanon, 67
   as refugees from Israel, 53, 54–55, 61.
   See also Palestine Liberation Organization
Paramount Studios, and Abdullah II on set, 78–79
Persia (Iran), and Great Britain, 30
Petra, 26
Philby, H. St. John, 46
Picot, François Georges, 30–31
   and Sykes-Picot Agreement, 30–31, 34
political parties, and Hussein, 72
prime minister, and Abdullah II, 91–92
primogeniture, 19
privatization, and Abdullah II, 92–93

Qualifying Industrial Zone, 92

Rabin, Yitzhak, 77–78
Radio Monte Carlo, 14

INDEX

Ragheb, Ali Abu Al-, 92
Raiyah, Princess (stepsister), 16
Ramle, 53
Rania, Queen (wife), 84–86, 90–91, 95
Rashid, Prince (cousin), 17
Rawabdeh, Abdul Rauf al-, 91
Reagan, Ronald, 72
Red Sea, 23, 50, 92
Romans, 22, 26
Royal Hussars, Abdullah II as Reconnaissance Troop Leader in, 70
Royal Jordanian Airforce, and Abdullah II in Anti-Tank Wing, 73
Royal Jordanian Airline, 92
Royal Military Academy at Sandhurst (Great Britain)
    Abdullah II attending, 70, 71
    Hussein attending, 59
    Talal attending, 56

St. Edmund's School (Surrey, England), Abdullah II attending, 64, 69
Salma, Princess (daughter), 84
Samaria, 53
Samu, 65
San Remo Conference, 34
Satloff, Robert, 84
Saudi Arabia
    creation of, 47
    and Gulf War, 75
    and Jordan, 24, 62, 104
Saudis
    and Abdullah I, 36, 46, 51
    and Ibn Saud, 28, 36, 46, 47
September 11, 2001 attacks, 95–96, 100
Sharon, Ariel, 88
social security, and Abdullah II, 86
Socio-Economic Transformation Plan, 90

Sodom, 22
Soviet Union, and Abdullah I, 51
Special Forces, Abdullah II as commander of, 19, 78, 79
Suez Canal, 32, 43
Suez Crisis, 61–62
Sykes, Sir Mark, 30–31
Sykes-Picot Agreement, 30–31, 34
Syria
    and Abdullah I, 36–37, 50–51
    and Abdullah II, 86
    and Arab Revolt, 29
    and dam on Yarmouk, 93
    and electricity, 93
    and Faisal, 32–33
    and France, 30, 32, 34, 36–37, 44, 48
    and Great Britain, 29
    and Gulf War, 75
    and Hussein, 66
    and Israel, 51, 65, 72, 88
    and Jordan, 24, 62, 104

Talal, King (cousin), 17, 56–57
    and Constitution of 1952, 58
    and coronation, 58
    as king, 58–59
Talal, King (grandfather), as king, 18
Taliban regime, 100
Taoukan, Alia. *See* Alia, Princess (stepmother)
terrorism, and Abdullah II, 95–96, 98, 100
Throne Council, 59
Tiran, Straits of, 65
Transjordan
    formation of, 18, 24, 37–39
    as territory designated for Arabs, 41, 46, 49–50.
    See also Abdullah, King (great-grandfather); Jordan
tribes, and Abdullah II, 86

INDEX

unemployment, and Abdullah II, 86
United Nations
   and Israel, 53, 73
   and Palestine, 51
   and Palestine Liberation Organization, 74
United States
   and Abdullah I, 51
   and Abdullah II, 100–104
   Abdullah II attending school in, 65, 69–70, 73, 84
   Abdullah II's military training in, 73
   and Abdullah II's visit with Bush, 95, 96
   and Afghanistan, 100
   and Bush, 95, 96, 100
   and Hussein, 12, 13–14, 18, 21, 62–63, 76, 79, 81–82
   and invasion of Iraq, 75, 100–104
   and Israel, 72, 77, 77–78, 79–81, 92
   and Palestine, 51
   and trade with Jordan, 92

Wadi Araba, 77
Weizmann, Chaim, 33
West Bank
   and Abdullah I, 54–55
   and Abdullah II, 54, 105
   and Hussein, 63, 64, 65, 73–74
   and Jordan's location, 24
women, and Hussein, 72
World Economic Forum, and Abdullah II, 104, 107
World Trade Organization, 93
World War I, 24, 31, 32
World War II, 50
Wye River Accords, 79–81

Yarmouk, and dam between Jordan and Syria, 93
Yassin, Rania. *See* Rania, Queen

Zein, Princess (sister), 16, 56, 63
Zein, Queen (grandmother), 18
Zionism, 31, 33, 37, 48, 49

PICTURE CREDITS

page:

- 11: © *Maps.com*/Index Stock Imagery
- 13: © Getty Images
- 15: © Hulton-Deutsch Collection/CORBIS
- 17: © Getty Images
- 20: Associated Press/AP
- 23: © Dean Conger/CORBIS
- 38: © Getty Images
- 42: © Getty Images
- 45: © Bettmann/CORBIS
- 52: © Getty Images
- 57: © Getty Images
- 60: Associated Press/AP
- 67: © Getty Images
- 71: © Tim Graham/CORBIS
- 80: Associated Press/AP
- 82: Associated Press/AP
- 85: © Robert Landau/CORBIS
- 87: © Reuters/CORBIS
- 89: © NADER/CORBIS SYGMA
- 93: © Reuters/CORBIS
- 94: © Reuters/CORBIS
- 101: Associated Press, ROYAL PALACE
- 103: © Brooks Kraft/CORBIS
- 106: Associated Press/AP

Cover: © DESPOTOVIC DUSKO/CORBIS SYGMA
Frontis: © Reuters/CORBIS

ABOUT THE CONTRIBUTORS

HEATHER LEHR WAGNER is a writer and editor. She earned a Master of Arts in Government from the College of William and Mary and a Bachelor of Arts in Political Science from Duke University. She is the author of more than 30 books and has written extensively on the creation of the modern Middle East and the conflict between Israel and the Arab world.

ARTHUR M. SCHLESINGER, jr. is the leading American historian of our time. He won the Pulitzer Prize for his book *The Age of Jackson* (1945) and again for a chronicle of the Kennedy administration, *A Thousand Days* (1965), which also won the National Book Award. Professor Schlesinger is the Albert Schweitzer Professor of the Humanities at the City University of New York and has been involved in several other Chelsea House projects, including the series REVOLUTIONARY WAR LEADERS, COLONIAL LEADERS, and YOUR GOVERNMENT.